*Routledge Revivals*

# Parliamentary Democracy and Socialist Politics

First published in 1983, this book is concerned with the prospects for socialist politics in contemporary Britain, in particular with the limitations of political analysis produced both by Marxist socialism and the non-Marxist socialism of the Labour left. The author suggests ways in which socialist political analysis and strategic thinking should be reconstructed if socialism in Britain was to survive political as a force. The major Marxist debates on, and the limitations of, socialist politics under conditions of parliamentary democracy are examined, as well as what is involved in a politics of democratisation. The dominant forms of strategic thinking on the Labour left are also analysed.

# Parliamentary Democracy and Socialist Politics

Barry Hindess

First published in 1983
by Routledge & Kegan Paul

This edition first published in 2017 by Routledge
2 Park Square, Milton Park, Abingdon, Oxon, OX14 4RN
and by Routledge
711 Third Avenue, New York, NY 10017

*Routledge is an imprint of the Taylor & Francis Group, an informa business*

© 1983 Barry Hindess

All rights reserved. No part of this book may be reprinted or reproduced or utilised in any form or by any electronic, mechanical, or other means, now known or hereafter invented, including photocopying and recording, or in any information storage or retrieval system, without permission in writing from the publishers.

**Publisher's Note**
The publisher has gone to great lengths to ensure the quality of this reprint but points out that some imperfections in the original copies may be apparent.

**Disclaimer**
The publisher has made every effort to trace copyright holders and welcomes correspondence from those they have been unable to contact.

A Library of Congress record exists under LC control number: 8216152

ISBN 13: 978-1-138-28177-6 (hbk)
ISBN 13: 978-1-315-27096-8 (ebk)
ISBN 13: 978-1-138-28180-6 (pbk)

# PARLIAMENTARY DEMOCRACY AND SOCIALIST POLITICS

BARRY HINDESS

Routledge & Kegan Paul
London, Boston, Melbourne and Henley

First published in 1983
by Routledge & Kegan Paul Plc
39 Store Street, London WC1E 7DD,
9 Park Street, Boston, Mass. 02108, USA,
296 Beaconsfield Parade, Middle Park,
Melbourne, 3206, Australia, and
Broadway House, Newtown Road,
Henley-on-Thames, Oxon RG9 1EN
Set in Linotron Baskerville, 11 on 13pt
and printed in Great Britain by
T. J. Press (Padstow) Ltd
Padstow, Cornwall
©Barry Hindess 1983
No part of this book may be reproduced in
any form without permission from the
publisher, except for the quotation of brief
passages in criticism

Library of Congress Cataloging in Publication Data

Hindess, Barry.
Parliamentary democracy and socialist politics.
Bibliography: p.
Includes index.
1. Labour Party (Great Britain) 2. Socialism
—Great Britain. 3. Labor and laboring classes—
Great Britain—Political activity. I. Title.
JN1129.L32H56 1982     324.24107     82-16152
ISBN 0-7100-9319-5

# Contents

| | |
|---|---|
| Acknowledgments | vi |
| Introduction | 1 |
| 1 Marxism and parliamentary democracy | 15 |
| 2 Democracy and parliamentary democratic politics | 47 |
| 3 The Labour Party and socialist strategy | 85 |
| 4 Problems of political support | 118 |
| Conclusion: Socialism and electoral politics | 142 |
| Bibliography | 157 |
| Index | 161 |

# Acknowledgments

Many people have helped in the preparation of this book, discussing some of the issues that it raises or commenting on draft chapters and on the articles and papers from which the chapters have been derived. I am particularly grateful to Julian Clarke, Lorraine Culley, Jack Demaine, Sheila Goodwin, Paul Hirst, Phil Jones, Elizabeth Kingdom, Nikolas Rose and Sheila Smith.

Much of chapter one originally appeared in Alan Hunt (ed.), *Marxism and Democracy*, published by Lawrence & Wishart. Parts of chapters two and three are based on papers published in *Politics and Power*. I am grateful to Alan Hunt and Messrs. Lawrence & Wishart, and to the editors of *Politics and Power* and Messrs Routledge & Kegan Paul for permission to reproduce the material.

# Introduction

This book is concerned with the limitations of the political analyses produced by marxist socialism and the non-marxist socialism of much of the Labour left, and with the prospects for socialist politics in Britain today. The first two chapters consider general questions of political analysis under conditions of parliamentary democracy and the remaining chapters take up some of the implications of their arguments for socialist strategy, concentrating on the non-insurrectionary socialism of the Labour Party and trades union left. Perhaps the best way to introduce the arguments of this book is to refer to two others: first, my *The Decline of Working Class Politics*, which retains a certain notoriety, although it was published just over a decade ago, and secondly, *Marx's Capital and Capitalism Today*, a two-volume reappraisal of the marxist theory of capitalist economies by Antony Cutler, Paul Hirst, Athar Hussain and myself, published in 1977 and 1978.

### (i) *The Decline of Working Class Politics*

*The Decline of Working Class Politics* (hereafter: *Decline*) examined political support for and activity within the Labour Party and argued that there had been two interrelated processes of decline in working-class politics. One concerned the participation of working-class individuals in political activity and the other concerned working-class identification

## Introduction

as a reason for political activity. The two processes were connected, I argued, because the fall in participation of working-class individuals made the Labour Party less of a class party, so that its policies became less oriented to specifically working-class concerns, thus leading to a further fall in working-class participation. This argument was based on a sample of Labour Party branches in Liverpool which had shown that local parties in working-class and middle-class areas differed significantly in their personnel and in the political interests of their active members. I argued that these differences in interests reflected differences in the class composition of the local population and in social conditions, for example, in the character of the housing stock. As for personnel, figures on age and length of membership suggested that in working-class areas parties were unable to recruit and retain new active members and were, therefore, in a process of decline, while parties in middle-class areas were in a process of growth. The argument then was that these changes in party membership led to corresponding changes in the interests represented in city party policy-making, making the party less attractive to actual or potential working-class members and thereby leading to further changes in the pattern of party membership. Finally, I suggested that these changes at the local level corresponded to changes in the party nationally towards a more middle-class party, gradually less able to attract working-class members and support.

There are many problems with *Decline*, most of which need not detain us here. The most important points raised by critics concern the dangers of generalizations about British politics based on a study of Liverpool and the book's construction of a mythical golden age of Labour politics in which local parties sustained significant working-class activism (Baxter, 1972; Forester, 1976). There is much to be said for both objections, although too much can be made of the distinctive character of Liverpool politics. As for the golden age of Labour politics, what evidence there is of local party activity and membership

*Introduction*

does not support the view that branches in the working-class areas of British cities were quite the centres of political activism that my argument implied (Forester, 1976; Minkin and Seyd, 1979a). Two further weaknesses should be noted here, neither of which received much critical attention. The absence of critical comment on the first of these is particularly surprising, for the book ignores what are perhaps the principal channels of representation of working-class interests in the Labour Party, namely, those provided locally and nationally by the affiliated trades unions.

But the most significant weakness for the purposes of this Introduction concerns the sociological reductionism that *Decline* shares with so much analysis, marxist and non-marxist, of British politics. What is at stake here is the treatment of important elements of political life as if they were determined by social conditions quite independently of the activities of parties, trades unions and other significant political actors. I return in a moment to the ramifications of this reductionism in the arguments of *Decline*, but it is worth noting two other examples before proceeding. One is the treatment of the working class as having interests that exist irrespective of whether members of the working class recognize them as such, being determined essentially by their economic location. This conception of working-class interests is ubiquitous in left analyses of British politics. It implies that the working class is a political force that may react to what Labour or other parties do, but whose essential character is determined outside of politics. I criticize this conception of interests in chapter two below and we shall see in the following chapters that it plays a crucial part in existing strategies for a left Labour government. Of course such reductionism is by no means confined to marxism or the left. We shall see in chapter four that it is an important element in Anthony Crosland's analyses of Labour's electoral support in *Can Labour Win?* For a more academic example, consider John Goldthorpe's *Social Mobility and Class Structure in Modern Britain*.

*Introduction*

Goldthorpe is concerned with the concomitants of mobility, especially its implications for the prospects for egalitarian politics in Britain. What is so striking about this book is that Goldthorpe draws his conclusions while paying not the slightest attention to the organization of British politics and its practices (Hindess, 1981). This is sociological reductionism with a vengeance, analysing people's attitudes towards social privileges and inequalities as if they could be treated independently of the political work of parties, the media and other organizations, and the struggles within and between them.

Returning now to the argument of *Decline*, it treats local parties as representing political interests which differ according to the class composition of the local population and the social conditions in which they live. The argument is then that changes in the pattern of party membership have the effect of changing the pattern of interest representation in the party to the disadvantage of the working class, thereby shifting party policy away from working class concerns and leading to further working-class disaffection. Obviously differences in the character of the local housing stock or the extent of owner-occupation provide potential bases for the articulation of very different political interests in relation to local authority housing policy or the level of rates. The difficulty with the argument of *Decline* at this point is that it regards the interests articulated in the different areas as if they were determined independently of politics, as if they were unaffected by the political work of parties, trades unions and other political agencies. In this respect *Decline*'s conception of interests does not differ significantly from the one noted above. It is this conception of interests as determined outside of politics that underlies what can only be described as *Decline*'s romantic pessimism with regard to British parliamentary democracy. The argument, in effect, is that as the Labour Party has ceased to be a working-class party, working-class interests have been effectively disenfranchised. British parliamentary

*Introduction*

democracy is, therefore, a façade, serving to suppress working-class interests while presenting the illusion of free and equal participation in citizenship. I have something to say about the dangers and limitations of that mode of critique of democratic institutions in the first two chapters of this book. We shall see that something very similar is involved in the Leninist critique of parliamentary democracy as essentially inimical to working-class interests. The conception of democracy involved in left-wing proposals for democratizing the Labour Party is problematic for rather different reasons, but there is a similar conception of interests at work in the tendentious histories of the Labour Party as essentially a matter of leadership betrayal of working-class interests.

However, *Decline*'s reductionism is not restricted to its limited conception of interest formation, for it has important effects in the analysis of policy as a function of the pattern of interests represented in the party. In effect the party organization is regarded as a channel of transmission of interests to the level or levels of policy-making. At any level of organization, what is transmitted upwards is the resultant of the various interests represented at that level. Given that model of policy as expression of interests, it follows that changes in the pattern of party membership will be reflected in corresponding changes in its policy.

Now, the most striking feature of this model of policy formation is its naivety. In regarding policy as the expression of interests it gives the impression of a certain political realism while evading the problems of having to come to grips with the specific conditions in which policy formation takes place and the diverse ways they affect what policies emerge. The point here is not that interests play no part in policy formation, far from it, but rather that it is ridiculous to reduce the conditions of policy formation simply to the 'interests' that are supposed to be involved. There is an excellent illustration of this point in Lewis Minkin's *The Labour Party Conference*. Minkin presents a comprehensive account of the ways in

*Introduction*

which Labour Party policy emerges out of debates at Conference: the role of the Conference Arrangements Committee in structuring the pattern of debate and the effects of the compositing of resolutions on the policy decisions that are likely to emerge; the effects of tradition and 'Buggin's turn' in determining the membership of the Conference Arrangements Committee and numerous other positions elected at or by Conference; the various ways in which unions decide how their block votes are to be cast; and so on. The conditions of policy formation at the levels of local government or the PLP are obviously very different, and considerations of the practical problems and consequences of policy decisions loom rather larger than they do at Conference. But the same general point applies namely, that policy should never be regarded simply as the resultant or expression of the interests that are thought to be involved. I stress this point because *Decline* is by no means alone in its naivety with regard to policy formation. We shall see that a closely related and almost equally naive model of policy as expression plays an important part in much Labour left discussion of policy formation in the party.

Finally, I should point out an important difference between the objectives of *Decline* and those of the present book. Both discuss the Labour Party, but their similarity hardly extends beyond that simple fact. *Decline* was concerned with identifying processes of change in the Labour Party, providing a sociological explanation of them, and then bewailing what it regarded as their political consequences. The arguments of the present book have very different objectives. Political changes and the current state of the Labour Party are certainly discussed, and there is much in these that might be bewailed, but my principal concern is with the dominant forms of political analysis and strategic thinking on the British left. Within that concern my objective is not to develop *explanations* in terms, say, of political sociology or marxist theories of ideology. Rather, as the character of my discussion

*Introduction*

so far may have suggested, it is to develop a critique of significant elements of the left's strategic thinking in terms of its conceptual limitations and its inadequate response to current political conditions, and to suggest some of the ways in which socialist political analysis needs to be reconstructed. Where I refer to recent debates on the left or other developments in the Labour Party my comments should be read in the light of that objective. They are not intended to provide an exhaustive account of the debates or developments in question, but rather to bring out problematic features of the dominant forms of socialist political analysis or to indicate some of their unfortunate consequences for strategic thinking.

## (ii) *Marx's Capital and Capitalism Today*

This reference to socialist political analysis and strategic thinking brings me to the second book, *Marx's Capital and Capitalism Today* (hereafter: *MCCT*). Marxism is by no means the only source of political ideas on the left today, but it remains a major point of reference for socialist arguments about the character and problems of the British economy and the conditions of socialist political struggle. *MCCT* provides a fundamental reappraisal of the marxist theory of capitalist economies. Work on the book began with an attempt to develop the marxist analysis of the capitalist mode of production dominated by 'finance' and 'monopoly' capital. However it soon became clear that these last concepts were profoundly inadequate and, further, that far from constituting a useful point of departure, many of the central concepts and problems of *Capital* were obstacles to the kinds of work socialists need to undertake if they are to come to terms with the problems posed by modern capitalism. A short outline of *MCCT*'s main arguments is included here since they provide an important point of departure for the present book.

*MCCT* argued that three groups of concepts have had

## Introduction

serious disabling effects on marxist economic and political analysis. First, there is the category of value, with its associated forms of analysis of the distribution of the product and of the nature and determinants of the profits of capitalist enterprises. Our concern was not primarily to intervene in the various technical debates around marxist value theory or to replace an inadequate theory of value by another. Rather it was to challenge the theoretical ground of these debates and the ways that marxist economic analysis is conducted in terms of the category of value. Marxist value theory inhibits the conceptualization of circulation in a credit-money economy, confines the role of finance capital to the redistribution of surplus-value already produced, and precludes serious investigation of the range of determinants of capitalist profits. The critique of value, therefore, cleared the way for our analyses of modern monetary forms, the conditions of existence of different forms of capitalist financial institutions and their articulation into the financial systems of national economies. Second, there is the conception of the capitalist mode of production as a structured totality governed by necessary laws of motion. Here our concern was not so much with the technical debates around the 'law' of the falling rate of profit or the marxist theory of crisis as with the conception of society as a social totality in which such laws might be regarded as operating. This conception has dominated marxist discussion of capitalist social formations, with the result that the structures of specific national economies are dissolved as objects of investigation, appearing only as exemplifications of capitalism and its laws. The conception of necessary laws of motion has directed investigation of changes and developments in capitalist economies either towards the postulation of a generalized 'monopoly stage' of capitalism, characterized by its own specific form of the capitalist laws of motion, or towards the search for crises and other terminal phenomena as necessary effects of the capitalist mode of production. Neither has much to offer with regard to the kinds of investigations needed to inform socialist strategic thinking under contemporary capitalist conditions. The argument here is not that marxism is inadequate to the modern world because, as Crosland argued in *The Future of Socialism*, capitalism has changed since the nineteenth century. Capitalism has indeed changed, though not in quite the way Crosland suggests, and marxism is certainly inadequate, but it was inadequate even to the capitalism of nineteenth-century England. Our argument is that there are fundamental conceptual weaknesses in marxism's basic concepts, that these were weaknesses at the time *Capital* was written and that they have seriously undermined marxism's capacity to come to terms with subsequent developments.

Finally, there is the treatment of economic agents as personifications of economic functions, to which definite interests and world outlooks are ascribed. What is involved here is the idea that economic agents are human individuals and that all social relations are relations between human subjects, however much they may appear to take the fetishized form of relations between things. Marxism, therefore, shares with Weberian sociology a fundamental inability to conceptualize economic agents other than human individuals, for example, joint-stock companies. The critique of 'personification' therefore provided the foundation for our subsequent discussion of the forms and effects of capitalist calculation and their relation to the structure and organization of capitalist enterprises. The conception of agents as human subjects with definite given interests, together with the conception of society as a structured totality, play a fundamental role in marxism's sociologistic conception of classes as collective actors, constituted as such by their common given interests and necessarily represented in politics and ideology. To criticize marxism's conception of the social totality and its sociologistic conception of classes is, therefore, to undermine the conceptual foundations of marxist political analysis.

This last point is the most directly relevant to the

*Introduction*

arguments of the present book. Socialism is a political ideology based on the objective of constructing planned and non-commodity forms of production and distribution. Popular democratic socialisms go further and insist that these should be cooperatively organized and democratically administered. What is distinctive about marxist-socialism is that it regards itself as *scientific*, in contrast to the politics of utopian socialism, and therefore as providing a guide to political practice. The opposition to utopian socialism is entirely justified: socialism can be achieved only by political struggle against opposing forces. The construction of rationalistic social blueprints may have its place, for example, in highlighting problematic features of contemporary conditions and suggesting alternatives, but it is no basis for the investigation of the conditions which socialist politics must confront. The problem is with marxism's pretensions as a guide to political practice. These involve two fundamental elements. First, the structure of capitalism as a mode of production and its laws of motion generate both the economic conditions of existence of socialism and the political preconditions for its realization. Second, the fundamental political forces in capitalist society represent classes and their interests and they are polarized around the working class with its interest in socialism and the bourgeoisie with its interest in the maintenance of capitalist relations. The polarization may be complicated by the presence of other classes and other interests, the political and ideological hegemony of the bourgeoisie, the political fragmentation of the working class and so on. But in the final analysis the size of the working class guarantees a majority for socialism if only it can be made to recognize its interests.

Both elements are substantially undermined by the arguments of *MCCT*. Neither the workings of capitalism nor its crises can be relied on to provide the economic and political conditions of social transformation, and there is no necessary political majority for socialism given in the working class. Political support for socialism must be constructed on the

## Introduction

basis of existing political conditions, and what those are can be determined only by analysis and investigation. It cannot be deduced from the supposed essential character of capitalism. Socialists must come to terms with existing political concerns, organizations and forms of struggle, rather than rely on broadcasting a general political appeal to an imaginary working-class political collectivity. In the British context the conclusion to *MCCT* argued that this involved two points in particular. The first is the importance of the Labour Party and other organizations of the labour movement in providing a political space for socialist arguments and principles to intervene in British political life. The second is the need to come to terms with democracy as a medium and form of political struggle, accepting not only the dominance of parliamentary democracy, but also the role of popular democratic forms.

These two points provide the organizing framework of the present book, two chapters concentrating on questions of democracy and two on the Labour Party and socialist strategy. The first chapter examines the principal early marxist debates on the character of parliamentary democracy and its implications for socialist politics. I argue that both the 'revolutionary' and the 'reformist' marxist analyses suffer from a reductionist class analysis of political institutions and forces. The debates between them nevertheless raise important questions concerning relations between parliament and the electorate on the one hand and parliament and the state apparatuses on the other. These questions are taken up in the second chapter, which argues in particular that there is no necessary contradiction between parliamentary and popular democracy. Parliamentary and electoral politics are fundamental arenas of social decision-making and they provide important, if limited, means of supervision over the state apparatuses. Nevertheless, they have significant limitations, many of which cannot be remedied through changes in parliamentary and electoral procedures themselves. I argue

*Introduction*

that any serious concern with the extension of democratic control in our society must also be concerned with the development of extra-parliamentary organs of popular democracy. The conclusion to *MCCT* also stresses the role of popular democratic forms in creating a popular base and means of struggle for socialism. This is an important point with serious implications for the conduct of socialist politics, but I have not tried to develop these implications in the present book.

As for the Labour Party, my concern is with the principal forms of strategic thinking on the left. These are dominated by the idea of an inherent working-class majority for socialism. I argue that that idea has serious and damaging consequences for left analyses of Labour's actual or potential support, for its accounts of the history and structure of the Labour Party, and for its approach to party policy. A fundamental problem for any socialism that takes the dominance of parliamentary democracy seriously is how to win power for socialist politics under parliamentary democratic conditions, and in particular how to combine a principled socialist politics with an effective electoral and parliamentary presence. Unfortunately, the idea of an inherent working-class majority for socialism has allowed the left to evade that problem. One of the most venerable debates on the British left is over whether Labour can become a socialist party capable of realizing that inherent majority and thereby serving as a vehicle for socialist transformation. Several contributions to that debate are considered in chapters three and four. By far the most influential left positions within the Labour Party at the time of writing aim to transform it into precisely the kind of 'socialist' party that might be expected to appeal to that inherent majority, if only it were to exist. Since it does not, a more socialist Labour Party of the kind currently favoured by the left would face electoral disaster in both the short and long terms.

The idea that socialists should assess Labour primarily in

terms of whether it can become a socialist party in this limited sense is dangerously misleading. I have already suggested that socialists must come to terms with the fact that there is no necessary political majority for socialism given in the working class. Once that is recognized it follows that Labour should be considered not simply in its capacity as a potential vehicle for immediate political action, but also as an arena, or set of arenas, for socialists to work within. The Labour Party has always been a coalition of diverse political groupings and organizations, reflecting a variety of political concerns and ideologies, but it is not a socialist party in any strict sense. Socialism has been and remains an important component of Labour politics, but it has never been the dominant element in that coalition. The Labour Party is uniquely important for British socialists because of its electoral and parliamentary strength and its connections with organized labour. That strength and those connections provide a valuable space for socialist arguments and socialist principles to intervene in British political life. It would be a tragedy if that were to be lost. There is little to be gained in winning the Labour Party for socialism at the cost of further serious erosion of its electoral base, reducing it to a parliamentary rump and threatening its links with organized labour.

Socialists should indeed work to transform the Labour Party but they should also be concerned to carry its electoral support and the labour movement along with it. That will not be an easy task and it will not be achieved in a hurry. Given the manifest weakness of British socialism outside the ranks of Labour activists, it must involve the left abandoning the short-term pursuit of what it regards as a socialist Labour Party, and working to maintain the party as a broad coalition. Whether such an accommodation can be reached must also depend, of course, on the behaviour of the Labour right and (in January 1982) the signs are not entirely promising. But there is an important sense in which the left and right in the Labour Party face analogous problems. Labour's parliamen-

*Introduction*

tary representation depends on the party organization in the constituencies, which is overwhelmingly dominated by the left. In this respect the prospects for Labour maintaining an effective parliamentary and electoral presence depend on both the left and right learning to come to terms with the forces, interests and ideologies that make up the Labour Party.

# 1 Marxism and parliamentary democracy

In his Introduction to Marx's *The Class Struggles in France*, Engels celebrates the new methods of struggle developed by the German working class in making use of universal suffrage. Compared with other political systems, he argues, those based on universal suffrage have one inestimable advantage:

> that it accurately informed us concerning our own strength and that of all hostile parties, and thereby provides us with a measure of proportion for our action second to none, safeguarding us from untimely timidity as much as from untimely foolhardiness (Marx and Engels, 1970, p.660, henceforth *MESW*).

The machinery of the parliamentary state provides the working class with a weapon to use against the state and the class it represents.

> And so it happened that the bourgeoisie and the government came to be much more afraid of the legal than of the illegal action of the workers' party, of the results of elections than of those of rebellion (ibid.).

This new method of struggle, the mass party organized as an electoral force, has largely superseded the old-style methods of street fighting and the like. So:

> if we are not so crazy as to let ourselves be driven to street

fighting in order to please them, then in the end there is nothing left for them to do but themselves break through this fatal legality (ibid., p.666).

At the time he was writing, and ever since, the representative institutions of parliamentary democracy have posed severe problems for marxist theory that have never been satisfactorily resolved, problems of political analysis, of the characterization of arenas of struggle and the forces engaged in them, problems of democratic theory and problems concerning the movement from capitalism to socialism. The weaknesses of Engels's argument are clear enough: he confuses voting for a party with support for its long-term objectives, and his conception of the movement of transformation from capitalism to socialism is most ambiguous. On the one hand he presents the prospect of a progressive shift in the balance of state power with the growing strength and organization of the working class, and on the other he writes of the need to preserve our forces against 'the decisive day' (ibid., p.665), when other modes of struggle will presumably come to the fore. Thus his argument appears to invoke both a parliamentary-democratic and an insurrectionary transfer of power and, since the relationship between them remains unclear in Engels's account, it has been read as supporting the most diverse conceptions of the movement towards socialism.

The confusions and ambiguities of Engels's account have haunted subsequent marxist discussion. This chapter tries to clarify some of the points at issue by considering two of the most significant early debates on parliamentary democracy and socialism, concentrating on Kautsky's commentary on the Erfurt programme of German social democracy and Bernstein's critique, and on the debate between Lenin and Kautsky over the question of the 'dictatorship of the proletariat'. There are, of course, other important issues for marxists at stake in these disputes, for example, the theory of value, the agrarian question, laws of tendency, etc., but I shall be mainly concerned with the arguments over democracy and parliamentary democracy in particular.

My discussion of these debates is intended to bring out general problems with marxism as a theory of politics and to establish the weaknesses of both the 'revolutionary' argument that the parliamentary state must be smashed and the 'reformist' argument for a parliamentary road to socialism. We shall see that there are important respects in which all three positions discussed here face similar problems, especially with regard to the supposed relationships between classes and their interests on the one hand and the institutional conditions and features of parliamentary democracy on the other. Many of the issues raised in these debates have been obscured by a tendency to counterpose a marxist orthodoxy to various revisionisms. But the diverse arguments of Lenin, Kautsky and Bernstein do pose serious problems that are not simply a matter of Bernstein's or Kautsky's 'revisionism' or Lenin's or Kautsky's 'economism'. At this level the disputes are effectively concerned with the location of sovereign power and its representative character. I argue here and in the following chapter that once the issue of sovereignty is displaced it becomes possible to pose a number of important questions for socialists concerning the analysis of politics under conditions of parliamentary democracy and also in relation to our conceptions of democracy and democratization.

## I Kautsky and Bernstein

Kautsky's book, *The Class Struggle* is an extended commentary on the programme adopted by the German Social Democratic Party at its congress in Erfurt in 1891. It presents an analysis of the nature of capitalist society and its development and outlines the objectives of social democracy and the means by which they are to be realized. Kautsky argues that socialism is the inevitable product of capitalist development, because of the economic effects of that development and their political consequences. The economic tendencies of capitalism involve an increasing polarization, with the decline of the peasantry and urban petty bourgeoisies, the concentration of capitalist production, and the growth of the organized working class so that it finally encompasses a majority of the population. The political consequences follow from the irreconcilability of the interests of the proletariat and bourgeoisie:

> Sooner or later in every capitalist country the participation of the working class in politics must lead to the formation of an independent party, a labor party ... And, once formed, such a party must have for its purpose the conquest of the government in the interests of the class which it represents. Economic development will lead naturally to the accomplishment of this purpose (Kautsky, 1971, p.189).

The industrial struggle of the working class leads it to make political demands, for the freedom to organize and for the rights needed to make that effective, freedom of speech, of the press and assembly. 'These privileges are to the proletariat the prerequisites of life; they are the light and air of the labour movement' (ibid., p.185). Nevertheless, Kautsky argues that the highest form of political struggle is not spontaneously developed by the working class, but requires a non-utopian, socialist consciousness which must be imported into the working-class struggle from without. Left to itself the working class would not develop beyond trade union consciousness. Kautsky argues that it is necessary for the working class to engage in parliamentary struggle, not only because of its effects on government, but also because of what it does to the working class:

> This very participation of the proletariat proves to be the most effective means of shaking up the hitherto indifferent divisions of the proletariat and giving them hope and

confidence. It is the most powerful lever that can be utilized to raise the proletariat out of its economic, social and moral degradation . . . Besides freedom of the press and the right to organize, the universal ballot is to be regarded as one of the conditions prerequisite to a sound development of the proletariat (ibid., p.188).

Parliamentary and electoral struggle itself forges the political cohesion of the class.

As for the modern parliamentary state, Kautsky's argument is similar to that of many recent advocates of a democratic road to socialism. On the one hand the state is an instrument of the ruling class and on the other it is capable of transformation through parliamentary struggle. The state will never go further in relation to nationalization or any other measure than the interests of the ruling class demand. It 'will not cease to be a capitalist institution until the proletariat has become the ruling class' (ibid., p.110). But, while the state works in the interests of the bourgeoisie, parliament allows the working class to influence government activity. Parliament 'ceases to be a mere tool in the hands of the bourgeoisie' (ibid., p.188).

In fact the struggle of the working class should be directed both towards an increase in the power of parliament in the state and towards the increase in their own influence within parliament. In the last resort, he argues, the power of parliament depends 'on the energy and courage of the classes behind it and on the energy and courage of the classes on which its will is to be imposed' (ibid., p.187). The growing strength and political maturity of the working class means that sooner or later it will obtain a parliamentary majority and the ability to make parliament the dominant element in the state. The socialist transformation is then just a matter of time.

If the working class did not make use of its mastery over the machinery of government to introduce the socialist system of production, the logic of events would finally call some such system into being – but only after a useless waste of energy and time (ibid., p.191).

So, the socialist transformation of society can be achieved through a parliamentary majority backed by mass popular support. Kautsky has little to say about the process of taking power and, on the whole, he is content to say that, while the character of the revolution will depend on the circumstances in which it takes place, it need not be accompanied by violence or bloodshed. One thing however is clear, that socialism will be reached only through the political strength and unity of the working class. Kautsky is resolutely opposed to any attempt at gaining power through a broadly based alliance of the popular classes, the radical bourgeoisie, peasantry, intelligentsia and petty-bourgeoisie. In his polemical book against Bernstein (Kautsky, 1899) Kautsky argues that such an alliance is both dangerous and unnecessary. The Social Democratic Party represents the working class, but that need not prevent individuals from other classes joining or lending it their support. *Individual* non-proletarians are not a problem, but if the party tried to embrace other *classes* it would lose its unity and strength of purpose and the specificity of its objectives. For example, he argues that a party of the working class and peasantry must remain on the terrain of existing forms of social organization, especially with regard to individual private property in the means of production. But a party of the working class alone can, and eventually would, struggle for the transformation of the forms of property and social organization.

For Kautsky, the construction of a political majority for socialism is not a problem in the long run: the development of the capitalist economy will ensure that the working class will be an overwhelming majority of the population, and the experience of industrial, political and parliamentary struggle will weld them into an unbeatable socialist political force. The foundations of Kautsky's optimistic thesis that socialism is the inevitable product of capitalist development are attacked by Bernstein in a well-known series of articles and in his book *Evolutionary Socialism*. Bernstein argues first against the alleged tendencies of capitalist development invoked by the Erfurt programme: the peasantry and the middle classes were not disappearing, small businesses were not being eliminated and the industrial working class was far from being an overwhelming majority of the population. That meant that, at least for the foreseeable future, there would always be a substantial portion of the population, neither bourgeois nor proletarian, whose politics could crucially affect the chances of achieving any major socialist objective. Second, even among the working class, the rapid growth in membership and votes for social democracy did not necessarily indicate any great desire for socialism. There are many reasons why workers might vote for or join the social democrats without being committed to socialism. Bernstein uses the example of Britain to argue that capitalist industrial development does not necessarily lead to the growth of socialist consciousness among the working class. Third, he casts doubt on the present capacity of the working class to take over the organization of production. For example, citing the Webb's *Industrial Democracy*, he argues that producer cooperatives have made such a poor showing primarily because of the contradiction between their democratic character on the one hand and the need for differentiation of functions and subordination once the unit reaches a fairly modest size on the other. For any reasonably large unit of production cooperative management is impossible: 'it is simply impossible that the manager should be the employee of those he manages, that he should be dependent for his position on their favour and their bad temper' (Bernstein, 1961, p.119).

The implications of that part of Bernstein's argument for social democratic politics are clear. Rather than directing its politics towards the utopian goal of a fully socialist society the social democratic party should aim at practical and realizable objectives, at social changes leading in a broadly socialist direction. It was in this sense that Bernstein could write that the movement means everything for him and 'the final aim of socialism' is nothing. Furthermore, since capitalism is not working to produce an automatic political majority for socialism, the achievement of socialist objectives must depend on the construction of political alliances between social democrats and other parties. These implications are well known, although the character of the marxist response to Bernstein's work, concentrating on the defence of marxist theory or on Bernstein's epistemology, has tended to obscure the political point of his argument.

However, for our purposes it is more interesting to look at what Bernstein has to say about democracy. Notice first that he makes a clear demarcation between revolutionary and democratic roads to political power. Revolution may well be quicker in the removal of obstacles and the power of privilege, but its strength lies in its destructiveness. Parliamentary struggle and constitutional legislation are 'best adapted to positive social-political work' (ibid., p.218). In a parliamentary democracy 'the appeal to a revolution by force becomes a meaningless phrase' (ibid.). Bernstein argues that the achievement of democracy, 'the formation of political and social organs of the democracy, is the indispensable preliminary condition to the realization of socialism' (ibid., p.163). Indeed it is in support of that point that Bernstein quotes Marx's and Engels's well-known comment on the lessons of the Commune, namely, 'that the working class cannot simply take possession of the state machinery and set it in motion for their own ends' (ibid., p.156). For Bernstein, the crucial point about that state machinery is that it was not democratic. But the political situation of social democracy is very different from that confronting the Communards in that liberal democratic forms of political organization already exist. They may be limited, but they are capable of change and development: 'They do not need to be destroyed but only to be further developed' (ibid., p.163).

Bernstein offers what he describes as a negative definition of democracy, as an absence of class government, if not necessarily the absence of classes. That definition, he says, rules out 'the oppression of the individuals by the majority which is absolutely repugnant to the modern mind' (ibid., p.142). The central element here is universal suffrage, since *in the long run* that ensures the subjection of the state to popular control. I emphasize 'in the long run' because Bernstein insists that suffrage is no immediate panacea:

> The right to vote in a democracy makes its members virtually partners in the community, and this virtual partnership must in the end lead to real partnership. With the working class undeveloped in numbers and culture the general right to vote may long appear as the right to choose 'the butcher'; with the growing number and knowledge of the workers it is changed, however, into the implement by which to transform the representatives of the people from masters into real servants of the people (ibid., p.144).

As an example of this process he cites the Prussian anti-socialist law and its subsequent repeal. Bismarck used universal suffrage as a tool but 'finally it compelled Bismarck to serve it as a tool' (ibid.).

It is precisely because of this conception of the potentialities of democracy that Bernstein objects to the phrase 'dictatorship of the proletariat'. In an era of parliamentary democracy talk of the need for a *dictatorship* is anachronistic, it belongs to 'a lower civilization' (ibid., p.146). Far from being a dictatorship, socialism must be the self-organization of the people:

> If democracy is not to exceed centralized absolutism in the breeding of bureaucracies, it must be built up on an elaborately organized self-government with a correspond-

ing economic, personal responsibility of all the units of administration as well as of the adult citizens of the state (ibid., p.155).

The need for democracy in this sense is what Bernstein takes to be the principal lesson of the Commune.

There are several issues raised by these arguments of Kautsky and Bernstein to which we shall return in the subsequent discussion. For the present, however, it is sufficient to note the similarity in their assessments of parliamentary democracy, both as a necessity for the political development of the working class and as an instrument of popular control over the state. To be sure, Kautsky insists in his debate with Bernstein that the 'suppression of the individual' is by no means uncommon in modern states and that it is disingenuous of Bernstein to claim that practice to be 'absolutely repugnant to the modern mind'. And he strongly objects to Bernstein's characterization of democracy as the absence of class domination. Modern democratic states show no hesitation in suppressing strikes, trades unions and other organizations of the working class when they can get away with it. So the existence of democratic forms by no means renders the need for working-class supremacy superfluous (Kautsky also doubts the democratic character of Bismarck's Prussia – but that is another story). Nevertheless, for all the polemical force of these points there is little to choose between them with regard to the potential power that a parliamentary democracy is thought to give to a popular majority. This shared assessment of parliamentary democracy is one of the central issues in the dispute between Lenin and Kautsky, to which we now turn.

## II Kautsky and Lenin

In this section I shall concentrate on the general argument

over socialism and democracy in Kautsky's *The Dictatorship of the Proletariat* and Lenin's response to it, although the dispute between them over parliamentary democracy and the road to socialism can be found earlier – for example, in *The State and Revolution* where Lenin asks, apropos of Kautsky's replies to the revisionists: but where is the revolution? I shall not consider Kautsky's account of events in Russia after October or Lenin's attempts to show that it is a complete distortion. *The Dictatorship of the Proletariat* was written in 1918 as a direct attack on the practices of the Bolsheviks, criticizing both their seizure of power in the second revolution of 1917 and their 'dictatorial' method of government thereafter. What is at stake in Kautsky's view is the clash between 'two fundamentally distinct methods, that of democracy and that of dictatorship' (Kautsky, 1964, p.1.). He argues that the method of dictatorship is based on fundamental errors, that it cannot lead to socialism and that the working class can and must gain power by democratic means. Democracy cannot be regarded simply as a means to the end of socialism, for that conception suggests that other means might sometimes be appropriate. Modern socialism means 'not merely social organization of production, but democratic organization of society as well'. For that reason socialism without democracy is unthinkable.

Kautsky's argument is concerned first to show that socialism can be reached through democratic means and second to demonstrate the effects of dictatorship. In this chapter we are concerned mainly with the first of these, and with what Kautsky has to say about the nature of democratic politics. To show that socialism can be reached by democratic means, Kautsky repeats the argument of his *The Class Struggle*. Socialism is the inevitable product of capitalist development, first because the economic tendencies work to produce a working class majority, and second because the experience of economic and political struggle welds them into an overwhelming political majority for socialism. In Kautsky's view a parliamentary majority, backed by a determined popular majority, is sufficient to push through the socialist transformation of society. The only danger is that of a right-wing coup. But what that shows is precisely that the bourgeoisie have good reason to fear democracy – and therefore that the working class should defend it tooth and nail. In any case if the working class waits till it is strong enough to conquer power through democratic means, it would be extremely difficult for 'the capitalist dictatorship to manipulate the force necessary for the suppression of democracy' (ibid., p.9.).

Where Kautsky does go beyond his earlier work is not so much in the general argument for a democratic road to socialism but rather in what he has to say about the character of democratic politics. Democracy means majority rule, but, unlike bureaucracy, it also means civil liberties and the protection of minorities. These last are crucial since they provide conditions for political organizations to work out alliances and differences in an open way and allow for changes in the party of government. We will come back to the notion of a plurality of parties in a moment. For the present notice Kautsky's hostility to bureaucracy. Bureaucratic rule leads to arbitrariness, the suppression of minorities and general social and economic stagnation.

> It is, then, urgently necessary for the executive to be subjected to public criticism, for free organizations of citizens to counterbalance the power of the state, for self-government of municipalities and provinces to be established, for the power of law-making to be taken from the bureaucracy, and put under the control of a central assembly, freely chosen by the people, that is, a parliament. The control of government is the most important duty of parliament, and in this it can be replaced by no other institution ... The activities of the executive can only be supervised by another central body, and not by an unorganized and formless mass of people (ibid., p.26).

We shall see that Lenin evades this argument for a freely-elected central assembly. But notice two features of Kautsky's position: first, the claim that parliament is able to exercise effective control over government bureaucracy; and second, the way Kautsky opposes a central assembly on the one hand to 'an unorganized and formless mass of people' on the other, as if those exhausted the possibilities. I shall return to both these points in this and the following chapter.

Kautsky argues that no modern, i.e. capitalist, state can continue to withstand popular pressure for universal suffrage and that the struggle between classes for control of the state 'is especially manifested in the struggle over the character of parliament, that is, in the fight for the franchise' (ibid., p.27). Here Kautsky returns to the view that the class character of parliament is ultimately determined by the extent of the franchise.

The final point to notice in Kautsky's characterization of democratic politics concerns his distinction between parties and classes. In a democracy, classes may rule but parties govern: 'the strength of parties changes even quicker than the strength of classes, and it is parties which aspire to power in a democracy' (ibid., p.31). The discrepancy between the analysis of politics in terms of parties and analysis in terms of classes is covered first by an act of Marxist faith:

> the abstract simplification of theory, although necessary to a clear understanding of realities is true only in the last resort, and between it and actualities there are many intervening factors (ibid., p.31).

Second, it is covered by the idea that parties 'represent' classes:

> A party is not synonymous with a class, although it may, in the first place, represent a class interest. *One and the same class interest can be represented in very different ways*, by various tactical methods ... Above all the deciding factor is the

position in relation to other classes and parties (ibid., emphasis added).

He gives the example of the Liberal and Conservative Parties in England which represent the same class interest, but try to serve it through different alliances, with the working classes in the one case and the landed classes in the other. The problem with Kautsky's argument here is that if parties are thought to lie at a different level of analysis from classes, political alliances must be conceived either as between class and class or between party and party, but not between a party on the one hand and classes on the other. In effect Kautsky deploys the all-too-common marxist manoeuvre of giving parties an autonomy from classes with one hand and taking it away again with the other. It is precisely this sleight-of-hand that allows him to treat the electoral strength of a party as a measure of the strength of a class. The advantage of democracy for the working class is that it 'gives a clear indication of the relative strength of classes and parties (sic)', whereas, under absolutism, 'the ruling, as well as the revolutionary, classes were fighting in the dark' (ibid., pp.35–6).

Nevertheless, for all that it is not consistently developed, the distinction between parties and classes plays a further important role in Kautsky's argument against Lenin. It allows him to erect a clear distinction between the dictatorship of the proletariat on the one hand and the dictatorship of a party on the other. The former refers to the state of affairs in a democracy when the working class eventually gains power, 'a condition which necessarily arises in a real democracy, because of the overwhelming numbers of the proletariat' (ibid., p.45) – and it is in this connection that Kautsky, like Bernstein, refers to the lessons of the Commune. Since classes rule but do not govern, the dictatorship of a *class* cannot be equated with the dominance of a particular *party*. Thus, as a form of government, dictatorship is no longer that of the proletariat 'but of a proletarian party' (ibid.). And where there are several proletarian parties the 'dictatorship of one of these parties is no longer in any sense the dictatorship of the proletariat, but a dictatorship of one part of the proletariat over the other' (ibid., p.46).

It follows, in Kautsky's view, that there can be no reason to interfere with democracy when the proletariat is in the majority. Thus dictatorship appears to be necessary only when the proletariat is in a minority. Kautsky tries to show that the seizure of power by a minority is a disaster from the point of view of socialism, but his argument on this point does not concern us here. In any case, he claims, such a seizure is premature and unnecessary, for the development of capitalism will itself ensure a substantial working-class majority and the conditions for a democratic transition to socialism.

The main lines of Lenin's response to Kautsky's arguments are well known. Lenin argues that Kautsky grotesquely misrepresents the sequence of events relating to the congress of soviets and the dissolution of the democratic assembly, and that he also distorts the conditions under which sections of the population were excluded from the franchise covering elections to the soviets. It is not that aspect of Lenin's argument that concerns us here, but rather his analysis of parliamentary democracy, first his argument that popular, or soviet, democracy represents a higher form of democracy than the parliamentary assembly, and second, his analysis of the parliamentary democratic state as a form of class dictatorship.

On the question of dictatorship and parliamentary democracy Lenin accuses Kautsky of arguing like a liberal rather than a marxist in treating democracy as a non-class issue. Here Lenin follows the argument of *The State and Revolution* that the state is primarily a machine for the suppression of one class by another:

> never forget that the state even in the most democratic republic, and not only in a monarchy, is simply a machine

for the suppression of one class by another (*Collected Works*, hereafter *CW*, vol.28, p.369).

This means that every state is a form of class dictatorship and that Kautsky's counterposition of democracy on the one hand to dictatorship on the other is based on a fundamental error. A democratic state is a dictatorship and its democracy is always democracy for one class and against another. It follows that the form of democracy must change as one ruling class replaces another. The parliamentary form of state represents the rule of capital and, in fact, so Lenin argues in his speech entitled 'The State', 'the more democratic it is the cruder and more cynical is the rule of capitalism' (*CW*, vol.29, p.485).

How is the class character of parliamentary democracy assured? First, and most important, the state machinery is not neutral with regard to the class struggle. The real business of the state goes on, not in the representative assembly, but in the state apparatuses where the military, police and civilian bureaucracies function as a more or less unitary body in the interests of the ruling class. Here state power is conceived both as representing the interests of a class and as residing in particular state apparatuses and institutions. State apparatuses are the locus, the means of action, of state power and, far from acting as instruments of the will of the assembly, and through that, of the electorate, they act in the interests of the ruling class. It is precisely because state apparatuses are conceived in this way, as specific means of action of the power of a class, that they are also conceived as a primary focus of revolutionary action. To capture state power it is necessary to disrupt their unity, set one section of the state power off against another, and to immobilize particular organs of the state. Once captured, a new form of state must be constructed. The old state machine must be smashed and replaced by a state machine of a new type.

It is in this context that Lenin refers to Marx's and Engels's comments on the lessons of the Commune, namely, that 'the working class cannot simply lay hold of the ready-made state machinery and wield it for its own purposes' (*MESW*, 1970, p.285). Lenin's understanding of these lessons is in marked contrast to that of both Bernstein and Kautsky. For them, the primary lesson of the Commune is that democracy is an indispensable prerequisite for socialism; and in their usage that amounts to an argument for parliamentary democracy. The Parisian working class could not simply lay hold of the existing French state machine because it was not democratic: they therefore set about constructing a democratic state machine of their own. Lenin counters that interpretation with the argument that there is democracy and democracy. Where Kautsky or Bernstein talk of democracy in general they fail to distinguish between bourgeois or parliamentary democracy and popular or soviet democracy. The lesson of the Commune is not that the working class needs democracy in general, but that it needs popular democracy in particular.

The class character of democracy is also thought to be assured in two further ways. First, in capitalist societies the democratic rights of freedom of association, press, assembly, etc., in fact benefit the bourgeoisie through its ownership of the media, control over meeting places, money, and other resources. Second, the protection of the rights of individuals and political minorities in bourgeois democracies is a myth. Such recognition or protection is always partial and selective, favouring bourgeois parties, while on all fundamental issues the proletariat 'gets martial law or pogroms, instead of the "protection of the minority"' (*CW*, vol.28, p.245).

Now, we have seen that Kautsky makes precisely these two points in his polemic against Bernstein, and that he uses them to argue the need for working-class supremacy in the state. The political significance of money and property and the political partiality of state action are not in dispute between Lenin and Kautsky. What is disputed is the *potential* power parliamentary democracy gives to a sufficiently strong and determined popular majority – the capacity, in Kautsky's view, of parliament with the backing of the organized working class to push through the socialist transformation of society. It is not the character, the past and present practices of parliamentary regimes, that is at issue here but rather their potential for what can be achieved within them. Many of the arguments that Lenin advances against Kautsky have little or no bearing on that point. What is central to Lenin's position is the claim that the very organizational form of the parliamentary democratic state is basically inimical to the interests of the working class. Those interests can be served only by smashing that form of state and replacing it with something essentially different. One essence must be replaced by another.

Thus, to talk of a democratic and peaceful road to socialism using the procedures of parliamentary democracy is to confuse the issue. Even the most democratic form of state is a class dictatorship – and without class dictatorship there cannot be democracy for that class. Lenin argues that the extent of the franchise does not affect the dictatorial character of the state one way or another. What is crucial rather is the institutional forms within which the franchise operates. For this reason, he claims, the withdrawal of the franchise from the old ruling class and their allies after the revolution 'is not absolutely necessary for the exercise of the dictatorship, it is not an indispensable characteristic of the logical concept of dictatorship' (*CW*, vol.28, p.265).

The essentialism of Lenin's analysis of democratic forms is central to his counterposition of popular, or soviet, democracy on the one hand to parliamentary, or bourgeois, democracy on the other, and to his resolute hostility to any proposal to combine the two. This comes out most clearly in his 'Theses and Report on Bourgeois Democracy and the Dictatorship of the Proletariat', prepared for the First Congress of the Communist International in March 1919:

> The proposal indicates the complete ideological bankruptcy of the theorists who defended democracy and failed

to see its bourgeois character. This ludicrous attempt to combine the soviet system, i.e., proletarian dictatorship, with the National Assembly, i.e., bourgeois dictatorship, utterly exposes the paucity of thought of the yellow socialists and Social-Democrats, their reactionary petty-bourgeois political outlook, and their cowardly concessions to the irresistibly growing strength of the new, proletarian democracy (*CW*, vol.28, p.467).

The optimism of this last phrase is, to say the least, more than a little premature. But, leaving that aside for the moment, the all-or-nothing character of Lenin's argument is the hallmark of its essentialism. Where parliamentary democracy keeps the mass of the working people far away from the machinery of government, proletarian democracy brings them close to it. Where parliamentary democracy depends on a division of labour between legislature and executive power, proletarian democracy replaces both by 'a self-governing, mass workers' organization' (ibid., p.459). Where parliamentary democracy elects representatives once every several years, proletarian democracy can recall them on demand. And so it goes on.

> Only the soviet organization of the state can really effect the immediate break-up and total destruction of the old, i.e., bourgeois, bureaucratic and judicial machinery.... which is the greatest obstacle to the practical implementation of democracy for the workers and working people generally (ibid., p.466).

For Lenin, the crucial point about the Commune is that it was not a parliamentary institution.

Now, whatever the lessons of the Commune may be, one lesson of the Soviet experience is that the implementation of a popular democratic organization of the state is far easier said than done. The practical, political and organizational, problems of bringing the masses close to the machinery of government, of replacing the state bureaucracies by the 'mass-scale organization' of the working people, are immense, especially where popular organs of struggle have not already been developed in the many areas of state activity that are to be taken over. These problems must be compounded if parliamentary forms of representation and control over state apparatuses are rejected out of hand. That, of course, is precisely the issue raised by Kautsky's argument that 'control of government is the most important duty of parliament, and in this it can be replaced by no other institution' (Kautsky, 1964, p.26). However limited the effectiveness of parliamentary control may be, there is a point to Kautsky's argument that is evaded in Lenin's essentialist rejection of parliamentary institutions as a form of bourgeois dictatorship. It is all very well to talk of dispensing with parliamentary-bureaucratic forms of state organization when some alternative forms of popular control and self-organization have been developed. Otherwise, it amounts to proposing that we dismantle even the limited form of popular control over the bureaucratic state machinery that parliament represents.

## III Problems in the marxist theory of politics and the state

The disputes over the relationship between classes and their interests on the one hand and the institutional conditions and features of parliamentary democracy on the other take us to the heart of the most fundamental problems of marxist analyses of politics, and they raise some particular problems concerning the analysis of politics in parliamentary regimes. We have seen that Kautsky repudiates Bernstein's characterization of democracy as the abolition of class government, if not yet the absence of classes, and that Lenin accuses Kautsky of ignoring the class character of democracy. It is important to be clear about the nature of these differences. At first glance the points at issue seem straightforward enough, and it would

## Marxism and parliamentary democracy

be all too easy to play Lenin, Kautsky and Bernstein off against each other: to note the essentialism of Lenin's account of parliamentary democracy and to argue with Kautksy, that the class character of the parliamentary state is not an all-or-nothing affair, that it could be utterly transformed by a parliamentary majority with the backing of a sufficiently determined popular majority outside parliament; or to argue, on the other hand, that Bernstein's account of democratic government, of its non-class character and its protection of minorities, ignores the entrenched position of capital in modern democratic societies and the fact that minorities are often given a very rough time in them. It would be all too easy, in other words, to present Kautsky as a reasoned exponent of the democratic road to socialism, avoiding the polar extremes of Lenin's essentialism and of Bernstein's revisionism. This may seem all the more tempting at a time when the diverse strands of 'Eurocommunism' are insisting on the necessity of a democratic road and have begun to distance themselves from the 'Leninist' theory of politics and the state.

Such an account would not survive close inspection – and nor would the rather different accounts required to erect Bernstein or Lenin as the hero. It is true that Kautsky avoids the economism of Lenin, but he does so only by erecting an economism of his own. We have noted his confusions and sleight of hand over the relations between classes and parties and his reliance on the economic tendencies of capitalist development to furnish an organized political majority for socialism. Or again, we have seen that there is little to choose between Kautsky and Bernstein over the power that parliamentary government gives to a sufficiently determined popular majority. The point of Bernstein's account of democracy as the suppression of class government is not to deny that the bourgeoisie may be well entrenched as a matter of fact, but rather to insist that that is not essentially built in to the structure of democratic politics.

The trouble with the game of playing these positions off

against each other, or for that matter against the diverse writings of Marx or Engels or Gramsci, is that it fails to consider what it is about marxist analyses of politics and the state that makes such disputes possible and so difficult to resolve. In marxist discourse problems of political analysis are posed in relation to a conception of society as essentially structured by the economy and, in particular, by the distribution of the population into classes with distinct and ultimately incompatible interests. Politics is then conceived as a sphere of representation of those interests and a crucial site of the struggle between them. This notion of representation is central: it means that classes and their interests are distinct from political organizations, state apparatuses and ideologies and yet are represented by them; that politics is fundamentally determined by the economy, by classes and their interests on the one hand, yet not fully determined on the other. It means, in other words, that there are features of political life not fully determined by classes and their interests. This is the point of the marxist slogans of determination by the economy in the last instance (but not before), relative autonomy, and the like. They try both to open a conceptual space for non-economic, non-class determinants of political life and to stop it getting out of hand.

Now, there is one crucial respect in which what is at issue between Lenin and Kautsky or Kautsky and Bernstein is the question not so much of the existence of this conceptual space, but rather of the precise location of its boundaries, and in that respect their arguments are little more than variations on a single theme. Consider first the Lenin-Kautsky debate. Politics, for Kautsky, is class struggle. The working class struggles first to obtain democracy and then to use it to effect the transfer of state power and the socialist transformation of society. Here democracy is more than a matter of universal suffrage since it also requires that the state apparatuses are subject to parliamentary control. And the strength of parliament depends on the balance between the classes backing it and those opposed to it. But, given the suffrage, the tendencies of capitalist development and the experiences of class struggle will ensure in the long run a parliamentary majority for socialism backed by a sufficiently strong and organized working class. Thus Kautsky presents democracy, first, as the product of popular sruggle, second, as ensuring the victory of socialism, and third, providing institutional conditions in which state power may be held by either the bourgeoisie or the proletariat. These institutional conditions can be conceived therefore both as representing the long-term interests of a class and as providing a neutral arena in which the classes contend for power.

However, it is this last point which leads Lenin to accuse Kautsky of arguing like a liberal rather than a marxist. Lenin maintains, as we have seen, that the institutional conditions of parliamentary democracy provide an arena of struggle that is in no sense neutral as between the contending classes. Parliamentary democracy with its periodic elections and division of labour between legislature and executive reflects the interests of the bourgeoisie. It must be overthrown and replaced by a proletarian democracy, the institutional reflection of the interests of the working class and working people generally. From this perspective it is clear that to argue, as Kautsky does, that power in a democracy may be held by the bourgeoisie or by the proletariat is to ignore essential class determinants of the institutional forms of political life. But, if the state and the institutional forms of politics essentially reflect the interests of a class, there is a sense in which political practices are not always so determined. To take an example that is especially pertinent in the present context, Lenin maintains that the practices of social democracy may, and sometimes do, fundamentally betray the interests of the working class. Those practices are determined, not directly by these interests but rather by struggle: in this case by the struggle between marxism and the varieties of revisionism, reformism and other tendencies that beset it. However much some of these tendencies may themselves be thought to represent the interests of classes, and Lenin clearly allows of other 'interests', e.g. of 'nationalities', the practices of social democracy are determined not directly by the interests themselves, but by the struggle between them, or rather between their representatives. Thus, although he draws the boundaries in a different place than Kautsky, Lenin's argument too requires a conceptual space for crucial features of politics that are not simply class determined.

We can now quickly consider Kautsky and Bernstein. In one sense, as I have suggested, there is little to choose between their analyses of the potentialities of parliamentary democracy. But Bernstein conceives of democracy as the absence of class government, a conception to which Kautsky is resolutely opposed. What is at issue between them seems to be the connection between classes and the forces engaged in political struggle. For Kautsky, those forces are classes or the representatives of classes – and we have seen some of the confusions this leads him into. Bernstein's position is less clear cut. Although he continues to refer to classes and their interests, and to the working class as a political force, it seems clear that he regards the movement towards socialism as not primarily a *class* issue at all. We have seen how Bernstein rejects the view that the tendencies of capitalist development can be relied on to produce a proletarian majority whose experience of struggle would weld them into an overwhelming force for socialism. It follows that if a political majority for socialism is to be achieved, it cannot be constructed simply out of the interests of the working class. It must rather be constructed through argument and persuasion, through the construction of alliances, till it embraces people of good will from all sectors of the population. This is the point of Bernstein's conception of democracy: it means not the suppression of government by one class and its replacement by another, but the end of class government as such. Instead government will be by political majorities constructed around programmes and objectives, and hopefully around the ethical ideal of socialism, not around the interests of classes. In this sense the forces engaged in democratic politics need not be restricted to classes and their representatives. But, the role ascribed here to ethical ideals is itself conceived as being a function of economic development.

> Modern society is much richer than earlier societies in ideologies which are not determined by economics and by nature working as an economic force. . . . in order to leave no room for misconception, the point of economic development attained today leaves the ideological, and especially the ethical factors greater space for independent activity than was formerly the case (Bernstein, 1961, p.15).

Here, non-class, non-economic determinants of social life are invoked but they are confined within bounds given by the development of the economy. For all his revisionism and his reassertion of an ethical basis for socialism, Bernstein does not completely break with the marxist conception of the ultimately determining role of the economy. What must be noted for our purposes is that his discussion extends the space for significant non-class, non-economic determinants of political life beyond the bounds set by Kautsky.

But, to return to the question of what it is about marxism that makes these differences at once possible and so difficult to resolve, there is a sense in which what is at issue between Kautsky, Bernstein and Lenin is a matter of variations on the single crucial theme of representation, determination in the last instance, relative autonomy, and the like. It is a matter of conceiving a relationship between the economy and politics, between the distribution of the population into classes on the one hand and political organizations, institutions and ideologies on the other, that is able to combine the ultimately determining role of the economy with the irreducibility of political life. Such a relationship must open a conceptual space for effective non-class, non-economic features of political life and keep them closely circumscribed: political life must be autonomous, but only relatively so. What is at issue, then, is not the existence of such a conceptual space but rather the way it is conceived and the precise location of its boundaries.

What makes these differences possible within marxism is simply that, for all the wealth of assertions that the economy assumes the fundamental role, but only in the last instance, and for all the diverse formulations of that idea, the precise mechanisms of the supposed relationship between economic 'base' and political 'superstructure' are nowhere clearly specified. 'Determination in the last instance' and all the other slogans are little more than a gesture towards a theoretical vacancy that always remains to be filled. It is because they are little more than a gesture that Lenin, Kautsky and Bernstein, and subsequently any number of others, can erect their different conceptions of the elements of political life that are or are not directly tied to class or economic determinations

However, and this brings us to the fundamental problem, it is not merely that this theoretical vacancy is left open. The problem is that it cannot be filled: the slogans of 'relative autonomy', 'determination in the last instance', and all the rest, are gestural evasions of a problem that cannot be resolved. There is no coherent way in which political life can be conceived as different from and irreducible to the economy and the distribution of the population into classes on the one hand and in which the economy is conceived as playing the ultimately determining role on the other. In this respect the positions of Lenin, Kautsky and Bernstein are predicated on somewhat different evasions of the same fundamental problem; and that is why there can be no resolution of the differences between them. Indeed the greater part of Marxist theoretical work on politics and the state consists of diverse and more or less sophisticated stabs at that problem and of interminable disputes between them. My co-authors and I have argued in *Marx's Capital and Capitalism Today* that that problem cannot be resolved, so that no proposed 'solution' can ever be more than gestural. There is no *general* mechanism of connection between the economic relations of a society, the relations between classes and whatever objective interests may be ascribed to them, and the formation of arenas of struggle in that society, the organization of forces engaged in them and the issues and ideologies on which they divide. There is no need to repeat our argument here and it will be sufficient merely to indicate the nature of the problem. Any solution must allow for elements of political life that are both effective and irreducible on the one hand and yet constrain their effectiveness to conform to the supposed ultimately determining role of the economic on the other. Now, it may be suggested that there are conceptions of relative autonomy that do not involve this difficulty. Indeed, some of our critics have made that suggestion, but none has come out with a developed concept that does the trick. Let me just say that the time is past when marxists could get by with the assertion of relative autonomy, that the onus is on advocates of this and other related concepts to establish the mechanisms of the supposed ultimately determining role of the economy, to show how they are effective rather than merely assert that they are.

To say that there can be no coherent conception of 'relative autonomy' is to say that the question of a relationship between political life and the economy that is able to combine the ultimately determining role of the one with the irreducibility of the other is wrongly posed, that we need to address a different set of questions. It is not to say that there are no connections between the diverse struggles to be found in modern society and the structure of its economy. Still less is it to say, as has sometimes been alleged, that politics is *absolutely* autonomous – whatever that may be thought to mean. It is to say that whatever connections there may be, there is no one general mechanism of connection between politics and the economy that is characteristic of capitalism as such – or, for that matter, of particular historical phases of its development. This is not, of course, to deny that conceptions of the interests of a class, and organizations claiming to represent such interests, may sometimes play a significant political role, or that certain business or financial interests may be well entrenched in the dominant forms of politics and the state. The point rather is that where such organizations or entrenched interests exist and are effective, it is as the outcome of struggle, perhaps of a series of struggles, to mobilize support around specific objectives, to defeat opposing attempts at mobilization, to establish particular organizational forms (in the Labour Party, in the structure of the NHS, or other state apparatuses) and so on – not of any necessities that may be thought to arise out of the character of capitalist economic relations. Unfortunately, the fact that so much marxist work on politics has been organized in terms of some gestural solution or other to the problem of a single general mechanism has had serious consequences for the way the struggles, the conditions in which they take place, and the forces engaged in them are analysed. Too often, marxist political analysis has the effect of neglecting the specificity of particular struggles and forces, and of relations between them, by dissolving them into classes, class factions and their supposed interests, while invoking 'anti-economism' or 'relative autonomy' to soak up any residue.

## IV The analysis of politics in parliamentary democratic regimes

Where does all this leave us with regard to parliamentary democracy? We are concerned with the forms and conditions of struggle in societies with parliamentary democratic forms of government, and with the options for socialist politics under those conditions. I have argued that political analysis conducted in terms of an imagery of economic determination and struggle between classes must be fundamentally inadequate, whether the imagery be that of Lenin or Kautsky or one of the numerous others available in contemporary marxism. The problem is not to establish the class character of democracy, to identify the class character of political forces, to construct alliances between classes and other interests, or whatever; it is to mobilize effective support around socialist objectives out of the forces, struggles and ideologies operative in particular societies. But to do that, we need to develop our analysis of parliamentary conditions of struggle. And this brings us back to another aspect of the Lenin, Kautsky, Bernstein debates for, although there is a crucial respect in which the differences between them amount to different evasions of an insoluble problem, what they have to say about parliamentary democracy is by no means reducible to these evasions. If we abstract from the imagery of class and economic determination which characterizes so much of the debate between them, there remain important issues to be considered in relation first to Lenin's counterposition of parliamentary and popular democracy and, second, to the analysis of parliamentary democracy itself.

On the first set of issues, it is clear that although Lenin represents the counterposition as one between a democracy that is essentially bourgeois and one that is essentially proletarian, his characterizations are not exhausted in that representation. It would take us beyond the scope of the present argument to discuss Lenin's notion of proletarian democracy at length, but it is worth noting a couple of points on what he presents as the polar alternative to parliamentary democracy. The first point is that, although they are critical of Lenin's essentialist counterposition of bourgeois to proletarian democracy, both Kautsky and Bernstein identify socialism with the development of what Bernstein calls 'an elaborately organized self-government' (Bernstein, 1961, p.155). There is no dispute over the conception of socialism as being fundamentally democratic, and over the consequent need to go beyond the limits of parliamentary democratic forms. Unfortunately, and this is the second point, what is involved in going beyond those limits remains remarkably unclear and, in Lenin's case, dangerously so.

It would not be too unfair to say that marxist discussions of popular democracy have barely advanced beyond Rousseau. What would the government of society as 'a self-governing, mass workers' organization' look like in, say, Lenin's Russia or in Britain today? As for the notion of 'recall on demand', proposed as an alternative to institutionalized and periodic elections, it is clearly unworkable for all but the most minute constituencies. Otherwise, it is in danger of being merely utopian. In a constituency of, say, 50,000 persons the notion of 'recall on demand' has no determinate meaning, except in terms of particular institutionalized forms of making that demand manifest. Suppose for example, that the voting machinery may be set in motion on receipt of the signatures of not less than a hundred, or not less than a thousand electors, then the effects of such a system of 'recall on demand' would depend on the minimum figure chosen. The alternative to a system of institutionalized direct elections is not the absence of institutionalization but some other institutionalized system: either a different system of direct election or a system of numerous minute constituencies such that the membership of central decision-making is effectively chosen by some indirect, but equally institutionalized procedure. Whatever the merits of different systems may be, it cannot be argued that parliamentary elections erect a division between the people and their representatives which 'recall on demand' is able to overcome.

These and other such slogans gloss over the considerable problems of integration and coordination of numerous distinct and internally complex political and economic practices – which would be the more acute if both parliamentary-bureaucratic and commodity forms of organization and distribution were to be excluded. I raise this point not in order to deny the possibility of popular-democratic forms of organization but rather, as I have already suggested, to indicate the dangers of any all-or-nothing opposition between parliamentary democracy on the one hand and popular democracy on the other and the scale of the problems that have yet to be resolved. We have to develop both our conceptions of what the democratization of significant areas of social life would involve and the organizational forms in which we could begin to realize it.

Turning to the analysis of parliamentary democracy, we have seen that both Bernstein and Kautsky, in rather different forms, regard parliamentary democracy as a means whereby the government of society may be taken into the hands of a popular majority, arguing that a popular majority can be translated into a parliamentary majority and that a parliamentary majority, backed by a determined popular majority, can subject the state machinery to its will. Leaving aside the question of the supposed class character of democracy, Lenin's attack on this position operates on two levels, arguing first that the 'real business' of the state goes on in the bureaucracy rather than in parliament, and second that in capitalist society the conditions of electoral struggle are fundamentally distorted by money and property, control of the media and of meeting places, and so on.

It is important to be clear what is at issue here. The arguments of Kautsky and Bernstein reproduce many of the crucial features of a constitutional mode of discourse, that is, of a mode of discourse that is concerned to attribute sovereignty to the state and to a specific location within it, so that other elements of the state may be conceived as agencies of the sovereign power. In effect, the argument is that parliament is, or may be, both sovereign and representative of the popular will. Lenin's response is not so much to question the pertinence of that mode of discourse, but rather first to question the location of sovereign power and its representative character (it does not reside in parliament, but in the bureaucracy and it represents the bourgeoisie not the popular will), and second to question the representative nature of parliament and electoral struggle.

This is not the place for a discussion of constitutional discourse and the theory of sovereignty, but it is important to register its effects with regard to the conception of the state as a unitary agency whose actions express the sovereign will. Rather than take the unity of the state as given, we should be concerned to analyse it as a specific set of institutions and arenas of struggle subject to definite internal connections and relations to other agencies and forces – and in some of his more practical political analyses Lenin does indeed attempt such an analysis. The following chapter considers some of the implications of analysing the state and parliamentary democracy in such terms. We shall see that there are important questions concerning relations between parliament and state apparatuses and the conditions of electoral struggle that are obscured in the sterile debates between Bernstein, Kautsky and subsequent advocates of a democratic road to socialism and their Leninist opponents.

# 2 Democracy and parliamentary democratic politics

I have used the debates over the supposed class character of parliamentary democracy and the possibility of a democratic road to socialism to bring out a major difficulty with marxism as a theory of politics. This difficulty results from what I and my co-authors have argued (Cutler *et al*, 1977) is an unresolvable problem reconciling a conception of the autonomy of politics, ideology and the state with that of the ultimately determining role of the economy and classes. Notions such as 'determination in the last instance' or 'relative autonomy' do not resolve the problem. They are, at best, gestures towards its recognition and at worst attempts to cover it over with a neat phrase. I have also suggested that the arguments of Bernstein, Kautsky and Lenin are by no means reducible to their various inadequate resolutions of that problem. They raise serious issues concerning the analysis of relations between parliament and the state apparatuses on the one hand and parliament and the electorate on the other, which I shall take up in the course of this chapter.

But discussion of democracy and democratization on the left is by no means hegemonized by those ancient and interminable marxist disputations. For some years now the Labour Party has been the site of often bitter disputes about democracy, in particular, about the relations between parliamentary democracy on the one hand and party democracy on the other. But the desirability of parliamentary democracy has not been at issue in these disputes and they have certainly not centred around its alleged class character. Democracy is now invoked on the left not only in the course of arguments for the need to improve on present forms of parliamentary control over the machinery of state, but also in relation to other spheres of social organization, notably the organization of work and the internal organization of the major institutions of the left, the Labour Party and the trades unions. This chapter examines how British parliamentary democracy works, its specific determinations and limitations, with a view to developing means of identifying limits on democratic control in Britain and of evaluating proposals for democratization.

First, however, it is necessary to say something about 'democracy', what is involved in saying where it exists, what its limits are, and so on. 'Democracy' is employed along with other concepts as a means of specifying certain of the conditions and characteristics of the mechanisms involved in reaching collective decisions, including the appointment of personnel (MPs, delegates, chairpersons, etc.). To say that a mechanism of collective decision is democratic is to say that it depends on a 'free' vote within some relevant constituency or constituencies, otherwise it is not democratic. To talk of democratic control over some set of decisions is to say that those decisions are made by democratic mechanisms. What the consequences of a democratic or non-democratic mechanism are will depend on its scope, how the mechanism is organized and the conditions under which it operates. In the case of a mechanism that is putatively democratic its scope refers to the range of decisions reached through that mechanism rather than in some other way. How it is organized covers such things as: the formation of constituencies, that is, those who may or may not take part in voting or discussion, which always involves some means of inclusion and exclusion; the way votes are aggregated to produce an outcome; conditions for initiating motions and for blocking them; rules governing a quorum; etc. But mechanisms of decision and appointment always operate under conditions that are not fully determined

## Democracy and parliamentary democratic politics

by their scope and organization. For example, in the case of parliamentary elections these conditions include: the policy and organization of parties and the character of the competition between them; the practices of other agencies affecting the electorate, trades unions, the media, churches, state apparatuses; legal and other constraints on effective freedom of organization and discussion; etc. The consequences of democracy are always dependent on the conditions under which it operates, and they are never reducible to the way the democratic mechanism itself is organized.

Now, it may seem that there is nothing unusual in this characterization. But it differs significantly from one that is still influential on the left which characterizes democracy in terms of an actual or potential relation between the supposed natural sovereignty of the individual and the effective sovereignty of the state. This difference is important first for the simple reason that consideration of sovereignty is normally linked to the state whereas, as we shall see below, there are good reasons why questions of democracy and democratization should not be restricted to the sphere of state or government decisions, and second because the notion of sovereignty involves severe difficulties which can significantly obscure political analysis. To talk of the sovereignty of parliament or the state is to conceive of the state as a unitary agency whose actions express the sovereign will. We have seen that an important area of dispute between Kautsky, Bernstein and Lenin effectively concerns the precise location of sovereign power within the state and its representative character. On one side is the view that parliament is or may be sovereign and that it can effectively represent the interests of the mass of the population, and on the other it is argued that, despite appearances, sovereignty rests with the state machine, the military, police and civilian bureaucracies, and that it represents the interests of the capitalist ruling class. In effect, analysis of parliamentary democracy in terms of a relation between the supposed natural sovereignty of the individual and the sovereignty of the parliamentary state can proceed in one of two possible directions. On the one hand parliamentary democracy may be presented both as a means of combining the natural sovereignty of individuals into the effective sovereignty of parliament and as a means whereby the citizens can control that effective sovereignty. This conception of sovereignty in the parliamentary state is influential in many Labour Party discussions of democracy and in marxist arguments from Kautsky onwards for a parliamentary democratic road to socialism. On the other hand there is the radical democratic critique of parliamentary democracy which sees in the relation between the natural sovereignty of the individual and the effective sovereignty of the state a problem of adequation, the inevitable discrepancy between the representative machinery of parliamentary democracy and the democratic ideal in which the people, or their interests or desires, are truly represented revealing the inadequacy of the machinery in question. Different versions of this approach can be found in Rousseau and in numerous socialist attacks on parliamentary democracy, from Lenin to guild socialism. Unfortunately, the attempt to measure existing 'democratic' machinery against such an ideal of democracy is utopian and ultimately destructive, for any system of democratic organization would be open to attack in terms of the problem of adequation. The radical democratic critique is a means of attack only. It provides no basis for concrete proposals concerning the modification of existing machinery or the specification of new democratic machinery to be constructed. We have seen the dangers of this approach in relation to Lenin's essentialist counterposition of bourgeois and proletarian democracy.

But it is the former conception of parliamentary democracy that is by far the more significant in contemporary discussions of democracy and democratization on the left. That conception has been clearly formulated in one of Benn's recent pamphlets.

## Democracy and parliamentary democratic politics

The parliamentary democracy we have developed and established in Britain is based, not upon the sovereignty of Parliament, but upon the sovereignty of the people, who, by exercising their vote, lend their sovereign powers to members of Parliament, to use on their behalf for the duration of a single Parliament only – powers that must be returned intact to the electorate to whom they belong, to lend again to the Member of Parliament they elect in each subsequent General Election (Benn, 1978, p.6).

It is because of this conception of sovereignty as loaned to MPs that even Benn, who in other contexts has done so much to emphasize the limitations on democratic accountability in British society, can write 'that all British Governments, Ministers and Civil Servants under their control, can only act within the laws of Britain and are accountable to Parliament for everything they do, and hence, through Parliament to the electors as a whole' (ibid., p.7).

What should be noted here is how such talk of the sovereignty of parliament obscures the simple point that in Britain, as in other parliamentary democracies, the vast majority of governmental decisions and appointments are not made by democratic mechanisms at all. The doctrine of the sovereignty of parliament involves the representation of other elements of the state, 'Ministers and the Civil Servants under their control', as if they were agencies of the sovereign power and accountable to it. So, although decisions of the state apparatuses are not in general reached by democratic process they are supposed nevertheless to express the democratically determined sovereign will of parliament, and therefore of the people. In this way it is possible to recognize the limited scope of democratic mechanisms in the British state in some contexts and deny them any significance in others. If we are to avoid such evasions, then investigation of the workings of a parliamentary democracy must consider what the scope of democratic mechanisms is and how it is determined. But we should also be concerned with the relationships between those decisions and appointments that fall within the scope of democratic mechanisms and those that do not. Democratic theory often represents those relationships in terms of a distinction between the making of policy and its execution, with the former being considered the primary focus of democratic concern. Such an approach makes perfect sense in terms of a theory of sovereignty, where the practices of all other elements of the state machinery are regarded as the more or less adequate expressions of the will of the sovereign power. Otherwise it is indefensible. It is the relationships between what falls within the scope of democratic mechanisms and what does not that provides the space for the intervention of other determinants of the practices of the state apparatuses. What those other determinants are and how they intervene are matters of major importance for any discussion of the strengths and limitations of parliamentary democracy.

Now, the importance of refusing to link the concept of democracy to any notion of sovereignty is that it opens up the possibility of assessing any putatively democratic mechanism in terms of its specific determinations and limitations by identifying first its scope and how that scope is determined and second, the way it is organized and other conditions under which it operates, and third, the identifiable constraints on discussion and voting, limitations of scope, and other effects which they impose. Not only does this conception of democracy displace the utopian critique, but the invitation to investigate the effects of the conditions under which a democratic mechanism operates leaves little room for any kind of complacency with regard to the workings of the British parliamentary system. It certainly leaves no room for the complacency that clearly underlies those Labour objections to proposals to subject the parliamentary Labour Party and its members to greater democratic control on the rather curious grounds, at least for members of the Labour Party to advance, that a more democratic Labour Party would pose a serious threat to parliamentary democracy as we know it. (See, for example, *Guardian* articles by Shirley Williams, well before she left the party, and by Michael Foot just before the deputy leadership elections: Williams, 1979; Foot, 1981).

But the assessment of democratic mechanisms in this way is inescapably complex and controversial, for there is no one dimension along which different mechanisms can be ranked simply as being more or less democratic. What properly falls within the scope of a particular mechanism or outside it, what are the relevant constituencies, how their boundaries are to be defined and how votes within them are to be taken (precisely what is to count as a 'free' vote?) and aggregated, and so on? Answers to these and other questions are necessary to any serious evaluations of supposedly democratic mechanisms, but they always involve a variety of considerations that cannot be derived simply from the notion of democracy. The consequences of democracy or democratization will always depend on how the various features of the democratic mechanisms interact with other conditions, and especially how they relate to the distribution of the social forces concerned with the decisions and appointments in question. For example, the Bullock proposals to extend democracy into the work-place would have brought democratic mechanisms into situations already structured by a distribution of powers and forms of organization involving management structures, unions, shop stewards, and a number of less formal groupings. The effects of industrial democracy would then have depended crucially on how the mode of organization of the democratic mechanism adopted related to that distribution of powers – as the opponents of 'single channel' representation clearly recognized.

So, democratic mechanisms cannot in general be subjected to a simple one-dimensional ranking, their significance always depends on conditions not given in the scope and organization of the mechanisms themselves, and different mechanisms may well have different consequences of substantive concern for the social forces involved. The argument here is not, as Jessop suggests (Jessop, 1980), that democracy should be regarded as a means that may or may not be appropriate to the pursuit of particular substantive ends. The point rather is that democracy is always a matter of particular institutional procedures and organizational forms. Their assessment is a complex matter in which the question of 'democracy' always appears in conjunction with a variety of other considerations. It follows that particular democratic mechanisms and specific proposals for democratization can not be assessed in terms of democracy alone. They should also be considered in relation to a politics, that is, a strategic assessment of current conditions and proposals in relation to some definite set of substantive concerns and objectives.

## Parliamentary democracy

In terms of the conception of democracy proposed here, parliamentary democracy may be described as a system of government in a public law form of state involving at least two kinds of democratic mechanism:

(i) democratic appointment to membership of a legislative assembly, and sometimes to other governmental positions (president, membership of local government authorities);
(ii) democratic decision-making within the assembly.

On this definition there are many parliamentary democracies in the world and many significant differences between them. But a few general points are nevertheless worth noting. First, we have already noted that in all cases the scope of democratic mechanisms in parliamentary government is extremely limited, for the vast majority of government decisions and appointments are not directly subject to democratic process.

Second, democratic mechanisms in a parliamentary democracy are always organized in particular ways with very particular effects. It is well known, for example, that the distribution of the electorate into constituencies and the way votes are aggregated can significantly affect the outcomes of general elections. The decision-making process in legislative assemblies is invariably hedged around with rules and conventions which constrain the kinds of interventions a member may make, the circumstances in which debates may take place and the conditions in which motions may or may not be considered. In many cases those conventions ensure that major decisions are effectively taken at one or more removes from any directly democratic process. For example, in Britain major government decisions are taken in Cabinet, a body whose members are not appointed by any democratic mechanism, whose organization is far from democratic, and whose deliberations are jealously guarded from parliamentary scrutiny.

Third, the mechanisms of parliamentary democracy always operate under conditions that are structured by a particular distribution of social forces and agencies. The appointment of members to legislative assemblies is structured in part by competition between parties which employ a variety of techniques for organizing the activities of the elected representatives. Parties differ according to their objectives, forms of organization and political calculation, and according to the elements of their internal organization that are subject to democratic mechanisms. All these features may be open to dispute within a party, and the outcome of such disputes can significantly affect the party's parliamentary or electoral practices. Numerous other forces and agencies, trades unions, financial institutions, employers associations and individual enterprises, the media, churches, parts of the state apparatus, and so on, intervene in the workings of the democrative mechanisms – and they may also be active in the space noted above between those decisions and appointments that fall within the scope of democratic mechanisms and those that do not.

These points are sufficient to indicate the dangers in any general theory concerning the significance of parliamentary democracy and the effects it may have. What the effects of electoral and parliamentary mechanisms are depends on their scope, how what falls within their scope relates to what does not, how they are organized, and how these elements interact with other conditions, forces and agencies. Parliamentary democracy cannot be regarded as a means of encapsulating some popular will in the sovereign power of the state, but neither can it be regarded as a sham whose representative institutions merely serve to mobilize consent for a power that lies elsewhere. The analysis of parliamentary democracy in terms of the scope of specific democratic mechanisms and the conditions in which they operate disposes of such simplistic myths. Instead it opens up the possibility of the substantive investigations into the workings of particular parliamentary democratic societies that are urgently required for a serious socialist politics of democratic social change.

## The scope of parliamentary democracy in Britain

The scope of a mechanism refers to those decisions and appointments covered by its operations as distinct from those made in some other way. In the case of parliamentary democracy we are concerned with at least two kinds of mechanism. I shall begin by considering the elected assembly and its relations to the state apparatuses and other spheres of decision, leaving consideration of the relation between parliament and people for later discussion. Consider first, the marxist debates around the position of parliament in relation to the state apparatuses. Lenin's position is clear: parliament is a talking shop and the real business of the state goes on behind the scenes. It is on this point, amongst others, that he accuses Kautsky of arguing like a liberal rather than a marxist. The accusation is unfair, for Kautsky's point is not that parliament does control the state apparatuses but that it can be made into a means of doing so: in the last resort the power of parliament depends 'on the energy and courage of the classes behind it and on the energy and courage of the classes on which its will is to be imposed' (Kautsky, 1971, p.187). Thus, for Kautsky, the growing strength and political maturity of the working class will eventually lead to the dominant position of parliament within the state. Abstracting from his confusion over classes and political forces, the argument is that the power of parliament within the state depends on the strength of the forces backing it as against those which favour other means of effecting state action.

Kautsky's argument has the merit of avoiding the worst effects of Lenin's essentialism since it assigns no essential character to the relations between parliament and state apparatuses and treats them rather as subject to variation and struggle. Unfortunately he gives no account of the mechanisms whereby parliamentary control is to be made effective or of the role of popular struggle in securing them. Kautsky's argument that parliament can exercise effective control, and Lenin's reply that it cannot, both concern the attribution of sovereignty, and they pay no further attention to the question of what the connections are between parliament and other state apparatuses or of how they should be analysed.

What is at issue is not just a question of pragmatic political analysis, of identifying arenas of struggle and the forces engaged in them. It is also a question of our assessment of the democratic character of the British system of government, considered not as a sovereign power but rather as a set of particularly significant spheres of social organization. In that sense the democratic character of a system of government is a matter not simply of its electoral arrangements but also of the effective relations between the elected assembly and the practices of the state apparatuses. I stress *effective* relations here since, once the question of sovereignty has been displaced, it is clear that what these relations are is not determined by their representation in constitutional discourse. It is particularly important to be clear what the scope of parliamentary mechanisms is, and to distinguish what falls within that scope from what does not. For it is the relationships between those two sets of decisions and appointments that provides the space for other determinants of government action to intervene. We have seen how the myth of the sovereignty of parliament is able to dissimulate the problem of these other determinants and their effects. The mechanisms of an elected parliament are not to be regarded as a sign, whose mere presence is an indication of moral rectitude, 'the good society itself in operation' (Lipset, 1960, p.403), or whatever, but rather analysed in terms of their effects. And those are crucially dependent on how the mechanisms interact with the other determinants of government action. In Britain, as in other parliamentary democracies, there are numerous limitations on the scope of democratic mechanisms, and there can be no question of attempting an exhaustive account of those limitations here. What follows is no more than a sketch of some of the more obvious ways in which the scope of British parliamentary democracy is limited. It is important to recognize that these limitations are by no means easy to overcome and that they cannot in general be dealt with merely by extending the sphere of direct government control.

(i) First there is the constitution, using that term somewhat loosely to refer not simply to what is specified in the forms of public law but more generally to features of state organization that are not readily altered by decision of the legislative assembly. In this sense the constitution is a matter of relatively enduring capacities of diverse state institutions and the relatively enduring pattern of relationships between them. Parliamentary democratic constitutions differ considerably but they all ensure that a variety of state institutions have a significant degree of autonomy from control by democratic mechanisms. In some cases, as with the US Supreme Court, that autonomy is strictly specified in public law. But there are other cases where there is no such clear legal specification of the capacities and relationships involved, for example the powers of the British prime minister and Cabinet and their independence of parliamentary control over many of their most important decisions.

Perhaps the best known examples of constitutional autonomy from democratic control in this country concern the position of judges and the institution of common law. Judges, recorders, stipendiary and lay magistrates are appointed by, or on the advice of, the Lord Chancellor who is a member of the Cabinet. These appointments are therefore formally subject to political control however much they may be, especially at the lower levels, effectively in the hands of the judiciary themselves and officials of the Lord Chancellor's department. Judges are appointed exclusively from the ranks of recorders and barristers. At lower levels recorders and stipendiary magistrates may be recruited from the ranks of solicitors. And even in the case of lay magistrates control over appointment is kept firmly within the legal system: outside bodies may be invited to nominate candidates but they cannot secure their appointment. Once appointed judges are not easily removed. Judges of the High Court and above may be removed only on petition of both Houses of Parliament – and none have been. Appointment to the judiciary is an important sphere of decision in British society that is subject to democratic control in only the most remote of senses. The same applies to the decisions made by judges and magistrates once appointed, and those decisions may well have an important political impact. This is not simply a matter of the well-documented tendency of the judiciary to reach decisions which restrict the rights of trades unions, students, women, and members of other categories, often against the clear intentions of parliament (Griffith, 1981, part 2). Judicial decisions may also significantly affect relations between government and private individuals or between different government bodies (as in the Tameside dispute over comprehensivization), and they may seriously limit the capacity of government agencies to carry out their statutory obligations. It was reported in July 1979, for example, that the chairman of ACAS had written to the employment secretary to say that the courts had made it impossible for ACAS to carry out its statutory duty to deal with trade union recognition issues (*Guardian*, 27 July 1979). The remoteness of judicial decision from any form of democratic control is further complicated in Britain, and in a number of other parliamentary democracies, by the existence of a common law tradition. In effect this is an evolving system of judge-made law based on the development and interpretation of precedent rather than on statute. This, too, has a significant impact on social life without being in the least subject to democratic control.

Another example is the autonomy of the Central Bank, which is characteristic of the advanced capitalist democracies. The governor of the Bank of England, and equivalent figures elsewhere, may be a government appointee but there are a variety of legal and institutional devices to ensure for the Central Bank a significant degree of independence from direct government control. Indeed, there are well-known cases where the Central Bank has deliberately subverted the policy of the elected government. Perhaps the most notorious example of this being the actions of Montagu Norman, Governor of the Bank of England, in sabotaging the Labour Government's attempts to raise a further dollar loan to bolster sterling in the weeks leading up to the formation of the 'National' Government in August 1931.

(ii) There are numerous instances of what can only be called a lack of extension of scope. Examples within the state sector include quangos, the widespread use of delegated legislation, and so on. A different kind of example concerns those areas of British society that are subject to regulation by private bodies whose decisions frequently have effective legal sanction: Lloyd's and the Stock Exchange; the Jockey Club; the professions of law, medicine and accountancy; and so on. The organization and content of legal education in Britain, for example, is still regulated by private bodies subject to no specific forms of direct statutory control. Or again, there are significant social policy issues where, within a broad framework of government regulation, major decisions are nevertheless left to private agencies. Titmuss argues, for example, that the power of private insurance companies means that 'social policies will be imposed without consideration of the moral consequences which may result from them, in this sense they will be irresponsible decisions' (Titmuss, 1963, p.216). A similar point could be made about Building Societies. I describe these in terms of a lack of extension of scope for two reasons: first, much of what is left to decision by private agencies in Britain is decided by statutory bodies elsewhere; second, because there is no constitutional obstacle to such extension. This is not to say that it would be easy to bring those areas within the scope of statutory regulation. On the contrary, in most cases that would require a major political battle. Nor, of course, is it to say that statutory regulation would of itself entail an extension of democratic control, for that would depend on the type of regulation adopted and on how it was organized.

(iii) More interesting for this discussion are the limitations given by the kinds of decisions that a legislative assembly is able to take, and their implications for the connections between parliament and the state apparatuses. To pose the problem of the connections between parliament and the state apparatuses is also to problematize the senses in which state apparatuses may be or should be subjected to parliamentary control. Notice, first, that it is too simplistic to examine these connections in terms of control or the absence of control. The radical democratic critique of parliamentary democracy has always insisted that the bureaucratic mode of government is itself a creature of the parliamentary separation of legislature from executive. This point can be found in Marx's commentary on the Paris Commune and in much of Lenin's writings on the state. The very separation between parliament, a body which issues decrees, laws and instructions, and bodies which are supposed to put them into effect both poses the problem of parliamentary control and imposes limits to its effectiveness. Consider the means of control actually or potentially available to parliament: issue of laws, decrees and instructions, questioning of ministers and civil servants, parliamentary committees of inquiry and investigative subcommittees, and so on. Simply to list the possible instruments of control is to recognize their limitations, to note the correlative opportunities for evasion and misdirection and the fact that no parliamentary body can hope to investigate more than a small part of the activities of the state. Contrary to Kautsky's attribution of a potential sovereign power to parliament, there are inescapable limits to the power of parliament within the state.

It would be absurd to pretend that any existing parliamentary assembly has even approached the limits of control that are in principle open to it. But what those inescapable limits show is that state apparatuses can never be reduced to the mere instruments of parliament's intentions. Nor are the limitations on parliamentary or ministerial control reducible to the political or ideological bias of civil servants, although that may well pose severe problems. To say that they cannot be mere instruments is to say that state apparatuses must be considered as, or as containing, political forces in their own right, subject indeed to constraints in the form of cabinet or parliamentary 'controls', but nevertheless with complex internal structures and relations with other state apparatuses and political forces generally. It is to say that state apparatuses or sections within them may themselves act on the conditions of struggle in parliament, cabinet and the electorate; that they may be subject to constraints and influences of various kinds from other state apparatuses and from forces outside parliament; that the effects of their actions cannot be reduced to the statutes they are supposed to enforce and instructions they are supposed to implement.

If we are concerned with the problems of extending democratic control in Britain then we must also be concerned to investigate the forms of organization of the various state apparatuses and their connections with each other, with parliament and with cabinet, the means of control presently employed and how they can be extended and, last but not least, the relations that exist between state apparatuses on the one hand and extra-parliamentary political forces on the other. What these relationships and connections are, and their political significance, cannot be deduced from the mere fact of parliamentary government. We must beware of easy generalizations about what may or may not be possible in Britain or anywhere else merely because there are democratic forms of government.

Finally, that there are inescapable limits to the power of parliament within the state means also that we should be concerned to develop other forms of democratic supervision and control over the state apparatuses involving, for example, wider public access to information, investigative journalism and forms of popular intervention in the functioning of particular state apparatuses. The point here is not to accept either Lenin's counterposition of parliamentary and popular democracy or, for that matter, Kautsky's counterposition of control by a central assembly to control by 'an unorganized and formless mass of people', as if those were the only alternatives. The extension of democracy requires that organs of popular control be developed, not that parliament be overthrown.

(iv) Finally, it is worth considering the implications of

capitalist private property for the scope of parliamentary democracy. This is important for two reasons: first, because an important part of the case for nationalization has been made in terms of the extension of democratic control, and second, because government economic management is dependent on the actions of legally autonomous capitalist enterprises. Within the Labour Party arguments for nationalization have usually involved one or more of the following elements. First, there is the argument that nationalization is needed to improve the efficiency and ensure the survival of particular industries that are clearly 'failing the nation' or in danger of doing so: that coal mining was inefficient because of its persistent low level of investment and its appalling industrial relations which could be improved only by getting rid of the coal owners; that the level of investment needed in the steel industry could not be financed from private sources; and so on. The second and third arguments concern the extension of democratic control in relation to two kinds of constituency. On the one hand it is said that nationalization removes the power to take decisions affecting the lives of thousands or millions of people from small and largely unaccountable groups of directors and transfers it to parliament, or rather to ministers who are accountable to parliament which is in turn accountable to the electorate. Part of the argument in *Labour's Programme, 1973* for an expanded public sector is this: 'It is intolerable that "the arbitrary exercise of economic power", as Tawney described the private capitalist system, should be permitted to frustrate the national will for full employment, regional justice and success in exports.' (p.30). Or again, 'if the causes of inequality are to be attacked at their roots, economic power must be transferred from a small elite to the mass of the people'. On the other hand it is suggested that the development of industrial democracy would be easier in a publicly owned, centrally controlled industry than in a multitude of enterprises dominated by the pursuit of private profit: 'The possibilities for experiment in industrial democracy in the (public) sector are considerable, and differ completely in scope from those in industry at large' (ibid.). The argument for efficiency and the national interest has been perhaps the most prominent, but there is nothing particularly socialist about it. Conservative as well as Labour governments have brought industries under public control for such reasons: for example, the nationalization of the electricity grid system and the constitution of London Transport under public control in the inter-war period and, more recently, the Heath government's salvaging of prominent 'lame ducks'.

But socialist exponents of nationalization in Britain have also emphasized the second and third arguments. The concern for public accountability through parliament has been the more important strand in Labour Party thinking, although the concern for industrial democracy has come to the fore in some sections of the Labour Party in the last decade. There are several problems with the argument for nationalization in terms of public accountability, but what should be noted here is that the representation of public ownership as an extension of democratic control depends precisely on the notion of the sovereignty of parliament. In fact it plays on both sides of that notion: first, ministers are accountable to parliament and thus to the populace at large; second, nationalized enterprises are agencies of the sovereign power whose actions can be made to express the sovereign will. To question the notion of sovereignty is to question the force of *that* argument for nationalization. It is far from clear that public ownership in any of its present forms involves any significant extension of democratic control.

Now, consider the question of government economic management. In advanced capitalist economies governments are significant economic actors in their own right, through fiscal and budgetary policy and through their spending and borrowing activities. Nevertheless the pursuit of many policy objectives requires that governments be concerned with the behaviour of capitalist enterprises and, with the exception of the nationalized industries, these are not government agents. Government management of the economy has therefore to be concerned with affecting the aggregate behaviour of a multiplicity of legally autonomous economic agents. Autonomy in this respect means that, as with other legal subjects, capitalist enterprises are subject to such general requirements as may be specified in law but they cannot otherwise be compelled or instructed to act as governments desire. Much as British governments, or the various 'Alternative Economic Strategies' of the left, ardently wish to increase the level of manufacturing investment there is no way short of major changes in company law that private firms can be *compelled* to expand their investment in accordance with those wishes. Even the nationalized enterprises are constituted as legal subjects with a definite corporate structure, thereby strictly limiting the ways in which governments can intervene in their economic activity. Bevan, for example, laments the 'statutory immunity of the boards of the nationalised industries from direct parliamentary control', which he regards as 'a constitutional outrage'. With some exaggeration he argues that it 'reduces the Minister to the status of either a messenger or an apologist for the boards. This was a mistake for which I must accept my share of responsibility' (Bevan, 1978, pp.127, 8). The point here is not that governments are helpless in the face of the legal autonomy of private enterprise or the corporate structure of nationalized industry, far from it, but rather that the legal constitution of enterprises constrains the kinds of actions governments may take in relation to their behaviour.

The limitations on government control imposed by the legal status of private enterprise are clearly recognized in the sections of *Labour's Programme, 1973*, dealing with Planning Agreements and the NEB. The *Programme* proposed a new Industry Act to give the government significant new powers in relation to private industry. Under the Planning Agreement system the government would secure information from the largest companies concerning 'such areas as investment, prices, product development, marketing, exports and import requirements' and those companies would enter written agreements to help the government meet certain clearly defined policy objectives, for example, by providing 'a certain number of new jobs in a Development Area' (*Labour's Programme, 1973*, p.18). The system was seen as providing 'a systematic basis for making large companies and enterprises accountable for their behaviour, and *for bringing into line those which refuse to cooperate – using, where necessary, the extensive powers under the proposed Industry Act*, as well as the activities of new and existing public enterprises and the powers of public purchasing (ibid., emphasis added). The *Programme* notes that the level of industrial investment 'has shown itself to be highly resistant to incentives, exhortations and the limited measures of control over private industry which are at the disposal of Governments' and goes on to argue for an extension of public ownership through the NEB:

> *only direct control, through ownership*, of a substantial and vital sector of the growth industries, mainly in manufacturing, which hold the key to investment performance, will allow a Labour Government of the future to achieve its essential planning objectives in the national interest. *An expanded public sector is a key instrument of the planning process* (ibid., emphasis added).

The force of this argument depends on the effective capacity of government to control the performance of enterprises in the public sector, something that, as the British experience has amply demonstrated, is by no means guaranteed by the mere fact of state ownership. For the rest, the fate of those proposals at the hands of the 1974 Wilson government (Hatfield, 1978, ch.11) reinforces the point made above that it will not be easy to significantly extend the scope of parliamentary control in this area. The attempt by Benn, Heffer and their working party at the Department of Industry to produce a White Paper embodying the *Programme*'s proposals was defeated in the Cabinet's public enterprise committee: the NEB was emasculated and Planning Agreements were no longer to operate on a compulsory basis.

This short account of some of the more obvious limitations on the scope of parliamentary control in Britain could easily be extended. What must be noted is that these and other limitations have no uniform character in terms either of their mode of operation or of the obstacles they pose. There is not an essential limit, of which the others are merely the diverse effects, but rather a dispersion of distinct and heterogeneous limitations. Some derive from the character of the division of labour between parliament and executive apparatuses, some depend on the particular constitution in which parliamentary mechanisms operate, and others are a function of the current lack of extension of scope and the consequent dependence of democratic mechanisms on the actions of other agents and forces. Thus, to describe a state as a parliamentary democracy is to say remarkably little about how the state apparatuses work, the major determinants of their actions, or what political forces operate on or within them. Answers to those questions require investigation of the state apparatuses in question: they cannot be deduced from the parliamentary-democratic character of the state still less from the capitalist character of the economy.

These limitations to the scope of democratic mechanisms structure the battleground in which a parliament or cabinet tries to impose its control and other agents try to resist or alter it. The capacity of ministers and civil servants to withhold information from parliament provide them with a simple means of evading parliamentary control. For example, the thirty-year rule restricting publication of minutes, papers and records of discussions ensures that many government decisions are subject only to limited parliamentary or public scrutiny. As Tony Benn has noted this type of government secrecy 'is based on the principle that accountability by publication is incompatible with good government and hence that democracy which depends upon accountability must be limited by a time gap of 30 years' (Benn, 1979, p.17).

For a different example, consider the now traditional complaint of Labour ministers, especially those on the left, that the political bias of senior civil servants disposes them to oppose their minister's policies and that civil service organization makes it all too easy for them to do so:

> In short, the power system in Whitehall is in no sense a democracy, but rather a mandarin-dominated bureaucracy with only limited ministerial control. If democracy is seriously intended, in the sense of electing a government with the effective power of enforcing its electoral pledge on the state officialdom, then this present power system requires a very radical overhaul (Meacher, 1979).

'Radical overhaul' is certainly needed, but this traditional left complaint exaggerates one problem and obscures another. That civil servants may successfully oppose their minister's policies is all too clear. But their opposition does not always operate against the left, or only against them. The attitudes of civil servants and the organizational means at their disposal constitute only some of the conditions of a possible struggle for control. They cannot predetermine its outcome. In some cases the policies of left-wing Labour ministers have been defeated by the overwhelming hostility of their Cabinet colleagues, and, in at least some other cases, it is difficult to avoid the conclusion that their own inadequate preparation was responsible for the defeat at the hands of their civil servants. One of the lessons that Benn draws from his experience as a minister is this: 'No Minister can achieve any significant change in policy unless he is able to work with his colleagues in Parliament or party or public who are of like mind and share his assumptions and his views.' He goes on to add that Crossman did not seem to grasp that point. His 'defeats always remind me of what might have happened at Waterloo if Wellington had forgotten to ask Blucher to send his troops in to help' (Benn, 1978, p.9). What the complaint obscures is the problem of what it is about parliamentary democracy that allows civil service resistance to develop and, at times, to be successful. It is not just a matter of political bias or of the particular forms of civil service organization and ministerial or parliamentary supervision – as if the limits to the sovereignty of parliament could be overcome by changes in personnel and organization. There is room enough for significant reform in all those respects. But what remains is the dependence of ministers and legislative assemblies on an executive apparatus for the implementation of their decisions. Particular features of that dependence may change but, whatever its detailed character, the forms of ministerial or parliamentary control will always be a matter of particular instruments of control, the limitations they impose and the obstacles that may be constructed against them.

## Parliament and the electorate

The other major aspect of parliamentary democracy that should be considered here concerns the relations between parliament and the electorate and the conditions of electoral struggle. Once again it is worth returning to the debates between Bernstein, Kautsky and Lenin, for many of the issues raised there have continued to haunt subsequent socialist discussion. Bernstein regards the right to vote as providing, in the long run, the means for transforming 'the representatives of the people from masters into real servants of the people' (Bernstein, 1961, p.144): and a similar view of relations between parliament and people can be found in many of the writings of Tony Benn. Now, that conception of representatives as, potentially, 'real servants of the people' involves a very limited view of the interactions between parties and the electorate. To the extent that parties are conceived as representing popular concerns they cannot also be conceived as determinants of what they represent. The activities of parties, therefore, reflect more or less adequately the desires or interests of 'the people', but play no significant part in the formation of those desires. In Bernstein's argument the electoral process appears simply as a means of aggregating the interests or wishes of an underlying population: different sections of the population may have different interests and/or wishes and these are brought together in elections and reflected in the relative strengths of parties and groups in parliament.

Kautsky has a different view of parliamentary democracy, but it is still seen as involving the subordination of government to a popular majority. The character of parliament reflects the extent of the franchise, and parties represent classes, so that their electoral support is a measure of the strength of the classes represented. The experience of economic and political struggle will lead the working class to the recognition that its interests are irrevocably opposed to those of the bourgeoisie, while the tendencies of capitalist economic development will ensure a working-class majority. Thus, in the long run, the numerical strength of the working class will be reflected in a parliamentary majority for socialism. Here, too, the electoral machinery is conceived as a means of aggregating popular concerns. While the activities of parties may have an impact on what those concerns are, the underlying tendencies of capitalism ensure in the long run that the expressed concerns of the working class correspond to their real interests.

So, in spite of their differences, Bernstein and Kautsky share a conception of parliamentary democracy as, in the long run, resulting in a situation where parties and groupings in parliament do represent the interests or desires of an underlying population. But the presumption of that long-run situation involves two further presumptions: first, that the votes of the electorate reflect interests and/or desires that are formed independently of the practices of parties and other agencies, and second, that these are effectively aggregated through elections. Lenin challenges both presumptions. Of course he does not dispute Kautsky's view that there are real or 'objective' class interests not dependent on party practices, but he clearly regards those interests as being fundamentally misrepresented and distorted in bourgeois democracy by the social distribution of money and property, control of the media, and other conditions of electoral struggle. The franchise and electoral machinery are likewise seen as rigged in favour of the bourgeoisie. Lenin also disputes the accountability of members of parliamentary assemblies, arguing instead for a system of recall on demand – and we have seen the utopian dangers involved in that part of his critique.

But the other points at issue in these differences between Lenin, Kautsky and Bernstein raise fundamental problems of the conceptualization of the field of electoral struggle. We are concerned with an electorate, organized into constituencies, whose votes are aggregated by an electoral machine to produce an outcome in the form of a distribution of seats to parties. How members of the electorate vote depends on a variety of external conditions and complex internal processes. The external conditions include the practices of other agencies, political parties, trades unions, industrial and financial enterprises, churches, media, sections of the state apparatuses, and so on, which do not vote but may nevertheless, as Lenin argues, significantly affect the pattern of voting. Now, what Bernstein and Kautsky represent as the long-run effect of parliamentary democracy requires us to envisage a situation in which the voting intentions of the electors reflect interests or desires that are formed independently of the practices of those other agencies. That idea has only to be clearly stated for its absurdity to become apparent: it requires either a realm of constitutive subjects endowed with free will and an autonomous capacity for rational calculation and decision, the unmoved movers of society and history, or else, as with Kautsky, it requires that class interests determined ultimately by the structure of the economy are able to override the distorting effects of these other agencies and their practices.

Now, that conception of class interests as structurally determined plays an important part in left analyses of Labour Party history and of the political strategy it should adopt, and its rejection is a significant component of revisionist counter-arguments. These positions will be discussed in later chapters. For the moment let me briefly try to bring out what is at stake in that conception by introducing a radically different conception of the ways in which 'interests', or talk of interests, play a role in political life. We begin by noting that interests are defined and articulated in the course of argument or evaluation. The point may seem trivial, but it has important implications for the ways in which interests may be said to have political repercussions. To say that interests are produced in the course of evaluation is to say that their definition is subject to dispute. Political conclusions derived from some assessment of what the interests of the working class are, are always open to being undermined by alternative assessments. In that respect arguments from 'interests' to political conclusions must always be regarded as problematic. Again to say that interests are the product of evaluation is to say that they are articulated by particular agencies, by individuals or by organizations such as governments, trades unions or political parties. The interests they articulate may be their own or those of others. Trades unions, for example, may calculate their own interests and those of their members, and they may also calculate the interests of various other constituencies, the labour movement, the working class, the unemployed, etc. Sections of the Labour Party, and numerous other left groupings may also claim to identify the interests of these constituencies. But there is no reason to suppose that the interests of, say, unions or their members as calculated by these various groups and organizations will necessarily coincide, let alone that they will correspond to the interests calculated by union members themselves. Indeed there are well-known cases where the politics of a union run counter to those of a majority of its members. An example that is particularly pertinent to Labour Party discussions of democracy is the decision of the TGWU executive in September 1981 to recommend voting for Tony Benn as deputy leader of the party despite clear evidence of majority support for Denis Healey from the union's own consultation process.

Now, the point of looking at interests in this way is that it indicates how the political repercussions of interests may be investigated. We begin with the calculations of interests (their own or others) by diverse agencies (unions, parties, factions, individuals) and with what they do on the basis of these calculations, and then consider the consequences of those activities. It should be clear that the working class cannot be considered as an agency in this sense. It does not calculate its interests and decide how to act on the basis of them, although there may be numerous individuals and organizations claiming to act in its name. It is only through the practices of those agencies that 'the interests of the working class' can be said to have any political significance. For example, the electoral consequences of the 1978-9 'winter of discontent', in which unions' assessments of their members' interests led them to reject the 5 per cent pay norm, followed from the economic and political ramifications of resistance by unions and numerous more or less organized groups within them. They are not the result of any reflex action on the part of 'the working class' to an unambiguous act of betrayal of its 'interests' by the Labour government.

The argument here is that interests do play an important part in political life, but only in so far as they appear as the product of some process of evaluation by particular agencies and as significant elements in their assessments of the conditions of action. 'Interests' do not function at all in the ways assumed by all too many left analyses. For example, we shall see in the following chapters that Labour's failure to represent what are said to be the interests of the working class is often used as an explanation of its failure to mobilize massive working-class support. The argument requires that the interests of the working class be identifiable as existing independently of the practices of parties and other organizations in order that they can serve as the standard against which the practices of particular organizations (the Labour Party, trades unions, etc.) can be judged. What makes it possible for interests to be seen as a standard in this way is that they are conceived as being inherent in the capitalist structure of the economy, so that they can be furthered only by a properly socialist policy aimed at transforming that structure. The claim is then that the Labour Party gains working-class support in so far as it appeals to those interests and loses it in so far as it subsequently betrays them or reduces that appeal (e.g. Cripps *et al*, 1981, ch.8). Because they are inherent in the structure of the economy, those interests exist whether or not significant sections of the working class recognize them. The argument, therefore, invites a thoroughly cavalier disregard for the long-standing evidence that the 'socialist' policies of the left have precious little working-class support. Precisely because they are conceived as existing outside of and above (or below) the practices of particular agencies it is impossible for this position to specify the social processes through which these interests are supposed to become effective. We will return at length to the dire consequences of that conception of interests as structurally given in the following chapters.

But, returning specifically to the field of electoral struggle, I have argued that the practices of parties and other agencies may significantly affect the pattern of voting – and there is no need to argue further, as with Lenin, that the net effect of these other agencies is to represent the interests of the bourgeoisie. To say that these other agencies may affect the pattern of voting is to say, first, that parties cannot be regarded merely as representing popular concerns, for they can also be significant determinants of those concerns, and to say, more generally, that electoral outcomes cannot be regarded as the product of the interests or desires of the electorate. They are the product of a complex play of forces in which electors themselves are never the only effective actors.

As for the aggregate character of elections it is clear that what is aggregated is *votes*, not the concerns of individual electors, and that electors may cast their votes in a similar way for a variety of different reasons. That point may seem trivial, but it has important implications. In particular, it means that the extent to which electoral outcomes reflect the concerns of the electors is not determined by the character of the electoral machinery as such. It depends rather on the character of the voting choices that are put before them, on the issues that are subject to debate within and between the competing parties. In this respect too it is clear that electoral outcomes cannot be regarded as the product of the interests or desires of the electorate. There may well be issues of widespread popular concern that are barely represented in electoral outcomes. The other side of electoral aggregation concerns its effects on the relative strength of the competing parties. It is well known that different ways of aggregating the same set of votes can produce widely different outcomes, that changes in electoral machinery can significantly affect the character of party competition, and there are well-known cases where governing parties have been known to gerrymander constituency boundaries in their favour. But we can register these effects without supposing that they necessarily emanate from the interests of the bourgeoisie.

These arguments pose problems for the way parliamentary democracy is often conceived. First, to say that parties compete in an electoral arena is hardly an adequate specification of the character of that arena or the parties and other forces active in it. The problem here is that to describe a form of politics as parliamentary democratic is to say very little about the political forces at work in the society or the sites of struggle and political issues in which they are engaged. Electoral and parliamentary arenas are by no means exclusive of other arenas of struggle or of significant non-electoral agencies acting on the various state apparatuses, parliament, and the electoral arena itself. What those agencies are and the effects they may have can vary considerably over time or from one parliamentary democracy to another, and it is impossible to assume that the electorate and elected assembly necessarily constitute the sole, or even the most, significant arenas of political struggle. It follows that there can be few worthwhile general propositions concerning the political effects of parliamentary democracy or the character of political struggle in democratic societies.

Notice, secondly, that electoral struggles always involve the play of diverse forces and agencies, that this is an inescapable feature of democratic politics. We have seen that parliamentary democratic government presupposes the existence of state apparatuses. Since they must be considered as, or as containing, political actors in their own right, it follows that, even if we leave aside the question of parties and other non-state agencies, there cannot be a parliamentary democracy in which the electorate is not subject to the play of non-voting but nevertheless effective agencies. It is impossible then to argue that the media or other agencies *distort* some presumably underlying set of concerns, for what the concerns of the electorate are must always depend on the actions of some set of forces or other. The distribution of forces may change but it cannot be eliminated. For similar reasons it is impossible to argue that the aggregative effects of particular electoral arrangements *distort* the wishes of the electorate. Different electoral arrangements have different effects, and we may wish to argue that some are preferable to others. But what those effects are will depend on the character of the parties and other forces at work in the electoral arena. They are never simply a product of electoral arrangements as such.

## Democratization

I have argued that the democratic mechanisms of a parliamentary state are to be analysed not in terms of their alleged articulation of the sovereign will, but rather in terms of their scope and organization and their interaction with other determinants of the actions of the state machinery. I have concentrated on showing how restricted the scope of parliamentary democratic mechanisms is in Britain, and on indicating some of the heterogeneous ways in which it is limited. It is clear that the bulk of decisions and appointments made within the state apparatuses lies outside the direct scope of democratic mechanisms, and that this restriction is by no means insignificant or unimportant in its effects. Of course, this is a problem in all Western democracies, and also in the socialist countries. To make these points is not to argue that parliament and parliamentary elections are an irrelevance, or that they are an ideological façade for bourgeois domination. It is merely to say that democratic mechanisms have a definite but limited scope within the state and that it is important to be clear what those limits and their consequences are. Parliamentary and cabinet decisions are only one set of determinants of the practices of the state apparatuses, and we should not assume that they are always the only, or even the most, important ones. But neither is it to argue that talk of the sovereignty of parliament is insignificant. The significance of political discourse is not restricted to its provision of a more or less reliable representation of, say, the workings of British government. For it can also function as an important component of political practice by providing some of the terms in which strategic calculation and debate may be conducted. Talk of sovereignty is a component in a number of important arenas of current British politics. It is used, for example: as a means of arguing for greater parliamentary control; as a means of presenting the civil service as a body of politically neutral administrators; as a means of campaigning against the compulsory reselection of Labour MPs by constituency Labour Parties; as a means of campaigning against EEC membership; and so on. The question of how it functions in these different contexts and the conditions in which it is able to do so cannot be considered here. But these examples will be sufficient to indicate that talk of sovereignty cannot be dismissed as nothing but a simple mystification.

What are the implications of these arguments for proposals for democratization and how they might be assessed and for considerations of political strategy and calculation under conditions of parliamentary democracy? The second set of issues will be taken up in the remaining chapters of this book, and I conclude this chapter with a few comments on democratization. Notice, first, that to locate talk of sovereignty as a component of particular arenas of political practice, rather than as a more or less adequate account of how they operate, is also to cut the ground from under proposals for democratization which presuppose the notion of sovereignty. We have seen, for example, that an important element of the traditional Labour case for nationalization has turned on precisely this idea of democratic control operating through the sovereign power of parliament and its ministers and through parliament's accountability to its electors. Similar arguments may be advanced for public control in other areas operating through national or local government. The point here is not to argue against nationalization or public control of other kinds, but rather to show that the case for extension of such control would have to be argued on other grounds. To argue that some of the limits to the scope of British mechanisms of parliamentary democracy are a function of their dependence on the actions of legally autonomous agents is not at all to argue that those actions be brought within the sphere of state control. The extension of the state sector transforms the problem of democratic control from a problem of control over legally autonomous centres of decision to that of control over centres of decision that are not legally autonomous – or not legally autonomous in quite the same way. Far from resolving the problem of democratic control, it merely changes some of the terms in which that problem must be posed.

However, to question the notion of parliamentary *sovereignty* is not to deny the importance of the democratic mechanisms of the parliamentary state. But in view of the heterogeneous character of the limitations on the scope of these mechanisms it is clear that a programme of further democratization cannot be limited to any one type of reform. In particular, it must involve at least two general categories of change.

(i) *improvements in parliamentary and electoral mechanisms themselves* – these might include: changes in parliamentary procedure; development of a system of powerful committees with sufficient resources to allow them to seriously investigate the behaviour of government departments and nationalized industries; subordination of Cabinet and prime minister to greater parliamentary control; constitutional changes; electoral reform; changes in the parties and other forces intervening in the parliamentary and electoral arenas; and so on.

(ii) *the development of non-parliamentary democratic mechanisms* – it is necessary to insist on this point because it can be obscured by notions of sovereignty. We have seen, for example, how Benn links the sovereignty of the people to that of parliament. Given that conception of the relations between parliament and the electorate it is all too easy to view the problem of democratic control over the state apparatuses as a matter for parliament alone. Thus Benn argues for '*a major shift of power between Government and governed through the strengthening of the role of parliament*, and the equipment of Members of Parliament with the necessary means for controlling Ministers' (Benn, 1978, p.17, emphasis added). There is a very strong case for strengthening the role of parliament along the lines Benn advocates, but democratization of the state apparatuses must also involve non-parliamentary democratic mechanisms. This is a direct consequence of the limits to the scope of parliamentary democracy in Britain discussed above, for we have seen that there are inescapable limits to the control of state apparatuses through parliamentary mechanisms alone. These non-parliamentary mechanisms might range from relatively straightforward devices, such as a comprehensive Freedom of Information Act and the abolition or substantial modification of the thirty-year rule, to non-parliamentary organs of participation in the running of the state apparatuses by their clients, employees and other constituencies.

Now, this reference to new democratic mechanisms returns us to the problem noted above that proposals for democratization can be assessed only in relation to a politics, a means of strategic assessment operating in relation to some definite substantive concerns and objectives. There are several issues here. First, conflicts between parliamentary and non-parliamentary forms of control over the state apparatuses are unavoidable. The latter certainly provide points of resistance to reactionary government policy, but they do so by providing points of resistance to government policy as such, whatever its character. Once new democratic mechanisms have developed there can be no guarantee that socialists will approve of the decisions they generate or that they will not conflict with decisions of a democratically elected parliament or local authority, just as the decisions of local authorities may sometimes conflict with those of the central government. Conflicts of this kind are an inevitable feature of a democratically organized society, and any extension of democratization must also extend the opportunities for them to occur.

It is precisely at this point that the doctrine of the 'ultimate sovereignty of parliament' may be invoked as a reason for not supporting the development of organs of popular control in the state sector, on the grounds that they would inevitably infringe on that 'sovereignty'. On this view, extra-parliamentary activity may be perfectly legitimate as a means of putting pressure on government, of demonstrating the strength of popular feeling on particular issues, and so on, or even, in some scenarios, as a weapon to be used in case of a right-wing coup. But the ultimate decision should always be left to parliament or the relevant local authority. The trouble with this view is that it fails to take account of the limits to parliamentary control over the practices of the state apparatuses and, more generally, of the limits to effective democratic control given by the institutional forms of parliamentary government. To argue against the extension of popular democracy in the name of the sovereignty of parliament is to say that democratic control should be confined within those limits. Consider what would be required if conflicts between organs of democratic control were to be avoided. There would have to be a single elected central governing body, aided perhaps by other elected bodies acting only within such powers as may be delegated to them from time to time. Decisions by the central body would have to be effected either directly by its own bureaucracies or indirectly by the subordinate elected bodies. To ensure that these latter do not conflict with the central body they would have to be closely supervised by the central government bureaucracies. Few capitalist democracies have achieved quite that degree of centralization, but the general character of this 'democracy' will not seem too unfamiliar: it is 'democratic' in the sense of having an elected assembly with the ability to pass laws and appoint governments, but it suffers all the limitations to effective democratic control that we have already identified in parliamentary systems of government. It does not escape from conflicts between distinct centres of decision; it merely ensures that those conflicts are between the assembly and sections of its bureaucracy or within the bureaucracy itself. Conflicts between organs of democratic control cannot be avoided without drastically reducing the level of democratic control that is possible in a society. Conversely, the possibility of conflict between parliament or elected local authority and organs of popular democratic control – say, over management of a housing estate – is a sign, not of the anti-democratic character of the latter, but rather that they represent a real extension of democracy.

Second, democratic mechanisms always have a particular scope, covering a certain range of decisions and appointments and not covering others, and they always involve a particular constituency or constituencies in a definite organizational arrangement. Thus, what counts as democratization may vary enormously depending on the scope, organization and constituencies involved. The importance of this point can be clearly seen in proposals for democratization of the health or education services, and the objections to them. In both cases there is dispute over the definition of relevant constituencies and the relative weights to be given to them, and consideration of scope has to confront not only the claims of a bureaucratic-administrative hierarchy but also the claims (albeit very different in their substance) to a professional expertise on the part of members of one or more constituencies. The significance of claims to professional expertise in these contexts (by teachers, doctors, nurses, social workers, planners) is that it provides the basis for a demarcation between a sphere of decisions that are 'technical' in character and therefore best left to the relevant specialists, and those that are 'political' in the sense that lay opinion may be acknowledged to have an important part to play. However, these various claims may be assessed, and even where a sphere of 'technical' decisions is acknowledged, there is clearly room for dispute as to precisely where its boundaries should be.

Third, democratic mechanisms operate in conditions that are structured by a particular distribution of agents, political forces and ideologies. The significance of democratization is never reducible to a function of the mechanism introduced. It always depends on the relationship between that mechanism and other forces and conditions. Compare the operations of the mechanisms of British local government in Northern Ireland before the imposition of direct rule from Westminster with those in the rest of the United Kingdom. Although the respective mechanisms were not identical, it is clear that the major differences in their operation were a product of the distinctive distribution of political forces in Northern Ireland. To take a different example, it was precisely the relationships between democratic mechanisms and other forces and conditions that was at issue in the minority report's objections to the Bullock proposals for single-channel representation. Should the representative machinery work, as Bullock proposed, through shop stewards and union organization, or, as the minority report preferred, should it be independent of them? The difference between these two proposed democratizations is important first because it would affect the resources, organizational experience and capacities at the disposal of the employee representatives, and second because the minority proposals aimed to significantly reduce the role of unions at the level of the workplace by assigning what would otherwise be issues for negotiation involving union representatives to the competence of a representative machinery that was not union based (Elliot, 1978). These examples show the dangers in assessing proposals for democratization without reference to the interaction of the specific mechanism proposed with existing struggles and forces.

Finally, it is important not to restrict consideration of new democratic mechanisms to the existing institutional structure, that is, to decisions and appointments presently being made, and how they might be democratized. The democratization of significant areas of social life may well require radical transformation of the scope of institutional arrangements in those areas. For example, democratization of the health services might also involve attempts to bring together those services provided at present through the DHSS with others that are the responsibility of the elected local authorities. Or again, the socialist objective of bringing significant elements of distribution under democratic control clearly requires the development of new forms of allocative machinery.

# 3 The Labour Party and socialist strategy

The remaining chapters of this book take up the implications of the preceding arguments, concerning political analysis under conditions of parliamentary democracy and the notions of democracy and democratization, for the principal conceptions of socialist politics in Britain today. They are concerned with the forms of non-insurrectionary socialist politics adopted by much of the Labour Party and trades union left and by the Communist Party of Great Britain (hereafter: CPGB). Although these positions differ in the detail of what a left Labour government (hereafter: LLG) would look like and how it might be achieved, they are united in the view that the primary objective of socialist strategic calculation is precisely the achievement of a LLG committed to implementing a series of radical policies, usually including what has become known as the left's Alternative Economic Strategy (hereafter: AES). There are many versions of the AES, ranging from a conventional reflationary package with some combination of import controls and devaluation to cope with its balance of payments consequences to more ambitious proposals to combine such a package with a radical restructuring of the British economy through planning agreements, expansion of the public sector and a major extension of workers' control. It is these more ambitious proposals that are generally presented in the context of a political strategy for socialist reconstruction. The AES is then presented not so much as an end in itself but rather as providing the preconditions for moving on to objectives even further removed from present conditions. It is often argued, for example, that the AES is not itself socialist but that its successful implementation would show that the left is capable of tackling Britain's economic problems, thereby winning 'confidence and support for the longer-term process of social transformation' (Cripps, *et al.*, 1981, p.132).

Now, there are serious problems with most versions of the AES considered simply as an economic package. However, my concern here is not with that aspect of socialist thinking, important though it is, but rather with the political analyses and conceptions of contemporary British conditions which can represent the achievement of a LLG armed with its AES as a viable objective of socialist strategy. These positions usually involve a number of interconnected themes concerning, *inter alia*, a history of leadership betrayal in the Labour Party and democratization as a means of combating it, and a belief in the existence of a mass base for socialism in Britain centred on the working class but extending far beyond it. The most influential socialist critiques of these LLG strategies in fact share many of their basic presuppositions, especially that of a mass base for socialism in Britain. Where they differ most strongly is in their assessment of the Labour Party, and parliamentary politics more generally, as a vehicle for socialist politics. One side sees the Labour Party as basically socialist, so that the problems of leadership betrayal can be overcome by introducing a proper structure of accountability within the party. The other side sees Labour as inescapably incorporated into the capitalist structure of our society where it performs the integrative function of containing and suppressing working-class resistance. From that point of view it is a dangerous mistake to imagine that the Labour Party can become an effective vehicle for socialist politics.

I argue that, for all their differences, both the LLG strategies and the predominant socialist critiques fail to come to terms with the conditions of British parliamentary democracy, and, in particular, fail to acknowledge the constraints and room for manoeuvre that current political and economic conditions provide for socialist politics. These constraints should not be regarded as immutable: conditions do change, and some of them may be changed through purposeful political action. But to achieve that, it is first necessary to recognize conditions for what they are. My argument is that many of the conceptions involved in LLG strategies and the arguments of their critics inhibit effective analysis of current conditions and the pressing political and economic problems that they pose, thereby allowing free reign to the elaboration of political and economic fantasy.

After presenting the main themes of the LLG strategies and their principal socialist critiques, this chapter proceeds to consider their consequences for political analysis, concentrating especially on the notions of democracy and accountability and the mass base for socialist politics that is supposed to be inherent in the structure of British society. To question these positions is to argue against the way the conditions of parliamentary and electoral politics are represented in LLG strategies, and to argue for a different approach to these conditions involving, in particular, a rethinking of the kind of Labour governments and policies that might reasonably be posed as socialist objectives. The following chapter continues the discussion of these issues, arguing that socialists have to be concerned, *inter alia*, with first, the furthering of policy objectives through government and, second, therefore with winning and sustaining electoral support. Current strategies of the Labour left are weak on both counts. The chapter examines left and right assessments of the relations between Labour and its actual potential electoral support and considers the prospects for improving its electoral position through changes in the Labour Party and the broader Labour movement.

## Strategies for a left Labour government

Consideration of LLG strategies is complicated for at least two reasons. First, there is the sheer variety of political positions, organizations and loosely organized groups that propose such a strategy: Labour Coordinating Committee, 'Militant', Rank and File Mobilizing Committee, 'Tribune' group, ILP, CPGB, and numerous others. There are no canonical texts and there is rarely any clearly specified theoretical basis, marxist or otherwise, for the strategy proposed. My argument here is largely concerned with positions that are widely shared by LLG strategies (and by many critiques) rather than with differences between them. For purposes of exposition, therefore, I draw a number of themes out of a composite LLG strategy, relying heavily for illustration on publications of the 'Bennite' Labour Coordinating Committee and the collective book, *Manifesto*, but referring from time-to-time to the CPGB and other positions.

The second complication is more difficult to explain. One of my arguments will be that LLG strategies involve significant elements of fantasy, including proposals that are clearly unworkable and often little more than the vaguest gesture towards some apparently desirable objective. But, supposing that argument were accepted, what follows? At one level very little. Consider, for example, the policy that Benn proclaimed as his first priority during the 1981 deputy leadership campaign:

> to restore full employment during the life time of the next Labour Government by adopting the alternative economic strategy (*Mobilise for Labour Policies*, Sept. 1981).

No one familiar with the state of the British economy can seriously imagine that even the most radical version of the left's alternative economic strategy will be sufficient to restore full employment. Are we then to dismiss Benn's policy as fantasy or, perhaps more generously, to regard it as a somewhat extreme but not otherwise untypical example of politicians' hyperbole on a par, say, with the extravagant claims regularly made by Labour and Conservative chancellors for their economic policies. Nobody, it might be argued, really believes what politicians say about the economy any more, so the hyperbole is merely a useful way of making a point; a proposal to eliminate unemployment is to be interpreted as a serious concern to reduce it. Perhaps – and it is certainly true that such extravagant claims are often tempered with *real politik* when their advocates are pressed. But it would be a mistake to treat the fantastic elements in LLG discussions as hyperbole and nothing more, for two reasons. First, however tempered by realism it may be, the fantasy can nevertheless close off any recognition of pressing political and economic problems. Returning to the example of unemployment, the fantasy of its elimination is sufficient to prevent any serious concern on the left with the problems of how to cope with the social and political consequences of continuing high levels of unemployment in British society.

The second reason is that the elements of fantasy are sometimes recognized as such and openly acknowledged as essential components of LLG strategies. Consider, for example, Geoff Hodgson's comments on the left's alternative economic strategy:

It would be a mistake to judge the AES simply by the adequacy of its inherent ideas, or by the ideas of those that support it. Instead, we should measure and evaluate the material force that the strategy represents. If the AES was backed by a mass popular movement, then that movement would assume its own dynamic and structures and push the leaders of the traditional Labour left well beyond the bounds of AES ... The fact is that the AES is one of the few points of leverage available to the left. The outcome of the battle within and outside the Labour Party between supporters and opponents of the strategy will materially affect the chances of creating such a mass movement in the 1980s. (Hodgson, 1979a)

The AES should not be assessed in terms of its coherence and possible effectiveness as an economic strategy, the assumption being that it probably would not be implemented and, if it is, then it won't be effective. Rather it should be assessed in terms of its supposed potential for popular mobilization. In effect, as many of its advocates affirm, the AES is really a *political* strategy. As an *economic* strategy it will serve to mobilize support, but the *cognoscenti* know better than to take it terribly seriously at that level.

Now, I have no doubt that most advocates of the AES are perfectly genuine in their support, but there are clearly elements on the left whose support is cynical or opportunistic. And that point applies more generally to LLG strategies: that is, they may well be proposed with little or no concern for their precise content or, say, their talk of democratization, or for their practicability as strategies, but rather for the political effects their proposal is thought able to generate. Underlying the strategy proposed, if we leave aside right-wing fantasies of Moscow gold aimed at disrupting the British economy or left fantasies of CIA funding of 'Militant' with the aim of disrupting the British left (why would they bother?), there is a rather different conception of what socialist strategy should be. In such cases there is little point in demonstrating that the strategy proposed is indeed of dubious coherence. But, as the extract from Hodgson's argument brings out very clearly, what is at stake here are conceptions of socialist politics not unlike some of those expressed in the LLG strategies themselves, especially the fundamental conception of an inherent but as yet unrealized mass base for socialist politics out there in British society waiting to be called into being. To the extent that they depend on such conceptions my critique of LLG strategies will be equally damaging to these more opportunistic approaches to socialist politics.

## The Labour Party and socialist strategy

The principal LLG strategies in contemporary British politics bring together a number of interconnected themes: a tendentious history of the Labour Party, contrasting its essential socialism with recurrent leadership betrayal; arguments for democratizing the party on the grounds that it is only their lack of accountability that allows 'Labour leaders to behave as socialists in opposition and as Tories in government' (*Labour Activist*, No. 7, 1979); arguments for left unity; claims that appropriate socialist policies are capable of generating mass popular support. Examination of these themes and their inter-connection will help us to identify the political analyses involved in LLG strategies. To question these analyses is then to undermine the principal LLG strategies and to open the way for a rethinking of the objectives that socialists might sensibly set themselves under contemporary British conditions.

### (i) A history of leadership betrayal

Why, ask the authors of *Manifesto*, has 'Labour lost much of its traditional support?' The answer, it seems, is 'because part of the movement, especially its official representatives and leaders, abandoned a class-based socialist strategy in favour of a compromise with the existing structure of power' (Cripps *et al*, 1981, p.105). The message is clear. First, Labour was originally class-based and socialist. Second, Labour's true character has been betrayed, but only by *part* of the movement, its leaders and official representatives, not by 'the party as a whole' (ibid., p.110) – and that betrayal has produced a significant loss of working-class support. These two elements, an invocation of Labour's true character and a history pointing to a fundamental divide between the movement and its present leadership, characterize a whole tradition of tendentious Labour Party historiography.

It is tendentious for several reasons. One concerns the alleged link between leadership betrayal and the loss of working-class support. I return to that issue below and in the following chapter. But two further reasons should be noted here. The first is that the evidence for Labour's true character is invariably highly selective and readily countered by evidence of other kinds. Evidence for Labour's socialist character is to be found in the vague socialist aspirations set out, for example, in Clause 4 of the party's constitution and reaffirmed from time-to-time in other such symbolic pronouncements. The existence of such pronouncements is beyond dispute, but what they establish is another matter. The Labour Party has gone through many changes since its formation out of the Labour Representation Committee over sixty years ago. But it has always been a more or less organized coalition of diverse political groupings and organizations, reflecting a variety of political concerns and ideologies. It would be difficult to argue that socialism, however understood, has ever been the dominant element in that amalgam. The Labour Party, together with the trades union movement, does indeed provide a space for socialist argument to intervene within the mainstream of British political debate, a space in which the appeal to socialist principles can still have a certain legitimacy and sometimes a limited effect. That space is important and valuable (compare the position of socialism in the USA) but its extent should not be exaggerated. To say that Labour provides a space for socialist politics is not at all to say that it is essentially socialist. It would be no less plausible to construct a history of the party as a reformist organization whose basic objectives are not so much to create a socialist Britain as to win seats in parliament and local government, to gain representation for the working class.

But the second reason is the more serious. The construction of a history of Labour as one of leadership betrayal of its true character requires a prior identification of what that true character is. Why is that a problem? Because it reduces analysis of a complex field of practices, objectives and interpenetrating arenas of struggle to a simple tale of an essential spirit combating alien infection. Once certain elements are singled out as defining the essential Labour Party, others must appear as incidental to it or else as alien intrusions. Thus, rather than investigate the ways in which Clause 4 and the like may be invoked as elements in diverse practices, debates and rhetorical pronouncements, they are placed, as it were, outside the analysis to function as a point of reference, a means of identifying deviation or betrayal within the party and of condemning other representations of it. Divergences between the essential party and other elements of the practices of the Labour Party then appear not as features to be analysed but rather as so many evidences of betrayal. In these histories such betrayal does not stand in need of explanation, except of the most perfunctory kind. Rather it stands apart as a subject for invective precisely because the history allows no role for the Labour Party other than realization or betrayal of its truth.

(ii) *Accountability and socialism*
In their submission to the Labour Party's Committee of Inquiry, the Labour Coordinating Committee conclude with five questions that should be asked of 'suggestions which claim to increase democracy'. The first is 'Do they make representatives more accountable?', and the last is 'Do they take us nearer socialism?' (LCC, 1980, p.23). If the Labour Party is essentially socialist yet betrayed by the party leadership then the fault lies in a party structure that leaves the leaders free 'to behave as socialists in opposition and as Tories in government' (*Labour Activist*, No. 7, 1979). The remedy is clear. 'We have got to get ourselves a system which makes the leadership accountable to the movement' (ibid.). The mechanisms of accountability to the rank-and-file tie individual MPs, the PLP and party leadership down, thereby providing the answer to the problems of leadership backsliding. That supposed link between party democracy and

socialist policies has been a recurrent theme throughout the campaigns for party reform in the last few years.

What should be noted here is that this argument for party democracy acknowledges a divergence between the 'real' Labour Party and other practices in the party – its leaders behave like Tories, its original socialism is in danger, etc. – and accord it the status of a betrayal. There is an impressive attempt to document this divergence in Lewis Minkin's *The Labour Party Conference* (1978). He examines the mechanisms and techniques of conference management in order to show that the apparent victories of the revisionists in the 1960s did not reflect any real conversion of the movement away from traditional socialist objectives. Whatever else they may have achieved the Gaitskellites had not 'won the post-war battle for the soul of the Labour Party' (Haseler, 1969, p.246, quoted in Minkin *op.cit.*, p.363). In Minkin's view the re-emergence of the left in Conference and NEC in the 1970s is to be seen as a development in which the gut feelings of the movement spring back after a period of repression.

(iii) *Left unity*

Although the Labour Party is seen as being essentially socialist, the left is disunited and therefore weak. The achievement of a LLG requires that this weakness be overcome. The classic British statements of the theme of left unity appear in the various editions of *The British Road to Socialism*, programme of the CPGB. The most recent edition points out that 'capitalism not only exploits people at work, it impinges on every aspect of their lives' (p.29). This fact, together with Britain's large working class, means that there is a 'political majority inherent in Britain's social structure' (p.34) for the Labour Party, which Labour has so far been unable to realize. Part of the explanation for this failure is to be found in Labour's right-wing leadership and the fact that the Labour left is simply not a cohesive and united force and other forces on the left are also disunited. Thus, a major objective of socialist politics must be to unify what is at present disunited. The Labour left in particular must develop links with extra-parliamentary forces and struggles, and it must be helped to overcome its disunity and lack of clear political perspective:

> The vital need is for an organisation of socialists, guided by the principles of scientific socialism, active everywhere among the people, in all the struggles, in all the unions, in all the progressive movements, and able to give leadership to them – in other words, an organised party, as distinct from the left groups in the Labour Party, the separate unions and the other social forces and movements (p.25).

The disunity of the left is to be overcome by means of an organization capable of overcoming that disunity. It is a problem of leadership. Hence the need for a stronger Communist Party and the equally clear but unstated need for others to fall in behind it.

Now, the role the Communist Party assigns to itself here is absurdly quixotic and there can be few outside the party's leadership who take that pretension seriously. But the underlying theme of left unity is a ubiquitous feature of LLG strategies. Thus *Manifesto*, with perhaps a touch more realism than *The British Road to Socialism*, (hereafter: *BRS*) assigns the unifying role to the new model Labour Party. 'The party now has the opportunity to draw together traditional and new bases of support' by adopting 'a class strategy' and appealing to all those 'oppressed by the shape of post-war society – especially women and the ethnic minorities and the elderly' (pp.118-19). Here, as elsewhere in LLG strategies, left unity is both presupposed and to be constructed, for it is their common oppression that defines what has to be brought together. The manifest and often bitter differences on the left over political concerns, strategic objectives and forms of political calculation are effectively reduced to the status of secondary phenomena, serving only to obscure the underlying commonality of interests which is ultimately supposed to constitute the unity of the left.

### (iv) *A mass base for socialist politics*

Finally, it is assumed that British society provides a potential mass base for socialist politics which could be realized by the left so as to sweep a LLG into office on a wave of popular support. This mass base is 'inherent in Britain's social structure' (*BRS*, p.34): it consists first of all of the working class and then, as a kind of supplement, everyone else who is oppressed by modern capitalism. This conception turns on a notion of working-class interests as determined by the capitalist character of the economy, and in that respect it suffers all the problems of the marxist positions discussed in chapter two. However politically divided and however uninterested in socialism they may appear to be, the working class are known to share a fundamental interest in the removal of capitalist exploitation that can be tapped for socialist politics. In effect, we know that 'class can revive as an issue that determines political loyalties' (Cripps *et al*, 1981, p.122). And, as if that knowledge were not enough, there is the 1945 election to comfort those who fear that socialist policies would risk alienating the electorate, thereby condemning Labour to years in opposition. Labour's 1945 election programme 'was the most radical in the Party's history':

> And where did all this lead? Did it frighten away the middle ground? History records that the 1945 general election ... resulted in the greatest victory in our history. The lesson is clear. (*Labour Activist*, No. 6, 1979)

It is always a bad sign when facts are presented and then left to speak for themselves, and this case is no exception. The greater part of Labour's 1945 programme, *Let Us Face the Future*, reflected the broad consensus which occupied the 'middle ground' of British politics at that time, and the bulk of its economic policies were the product of a tradition of

## The Labour Party and socialist strategy

reformist economic management developed on the right of the Labour Party in the second half of the 1930s (Addison, 1975; Pimlott, 1977). That such a programme could then attract massive support tells us nothing about the attractiveness of the present policies of the Labour left. In effect, this use of the 1945 election programme discounts the changes in British society over the last thirty or so years. What evidence there is of electoral support for policy positions suggests that left economic policies are unpopular even amongst committed Labour voters. The myth of 1945 allows those who invoke it to bask in the certainty of a popular majority for socialism in Britain today, in the face of all the available evidence. To return to 1945 is to turn away from the problems of the present.

The idea of a potential mass base is common ground in LLG strategies, and most now link the projected growth of popular support to the supposed appeal of the left's Alternative Economic Strategy. But there are significant differences concerning the role of mass support in the achievement of a LLG. A widespread view inside the Labour Party is that support must be developed in and channelled through the existing institutions of the Labour movement. But there is also an influential argument that the realization of a LLG and implementation of the Alternative Economic Strategy will depend on a more general, popular mobilization. This view can be found, for example, in Peter Hain's proposals for turning Labour into a mass party giving 'priority to extra-parliamentary action, even to the point of subordinating electoral politics to it' (Hain, 1981, p.192), and in several expositions of the Alternative Economic Strategy (Aaronovitch, 1980; CSE, 1980). But the classic formulation is again to be found in *The British Road to Socialism*:

> Mass struggle outside parliament has a vital role to play now and in the future – as a political educator of millions of people whose socialist ideas (sic) will be developed in such

struggle; as the essential means for ensuring that an elected Labour parliamentary majority does the job it was elected to do; and as the essential weapon for breaking the resistance of the monopolists and their political representatives. Indeed, *the major changes won throughout the history of the labour movement have come mainly as a result of struggle outside Parliament* (p.35, emphasis added).

The history of the Labour movement plays a similar role here to that of the myth of 1945 discussed above. Socialists are not now confronted with the political conditions of the past, and I shall argue below that this invocation of history is a way of refusing to come to terms with the conditions confronting socialist politics today.

## Socialist critiques of LLG strategies

Probably the most influential socialist critique of the LLG strategies is the argument advanced by Ralph Miliband and, subsequently, in rather different forms by David Coates and Leo Panitch to the effect that the Labour Party cannot function as an effective vehicle for socialist politics because it is incapable of mobilizing the working class for socialism. They share with the LLG strategies a basic concern with developing the policies and organization capable of triggering the socialist potential of the working class, but differ from them in their assessment of the Labour Party. Where LLG strategies present a history of leadership betrayal that can be overcome by introducing appropriate forms of accountability, the critique sees betrayal of working-class interests as an incorrigible feature of the Labour Party. Miliband, Coates and Panitch each offer their own version of the story, but the basic argument is that Labour occupies a contradictory position in British society. On the one hand it appears to represent the interests of the working class, while on the other it functions in the interests of capital to contain the inherent militancy and socialist potential of the working class. Labour's structural role in containing the working class and effectively suppressing its interests is masked by its union connections and by the socialist rhetoric of the Labour left:

> The Labour left has traditionally been and remains a bridge (and a much trampled bridge at that) between the rank-and-file and the Labour leadership ... It may be a nuisance at times; but it is nevertheless exceedingly useful to the Labour leaders. It helps to keep alive the myth of a transformable Labour Party (Miliband, 1976, p.133).

In Miliband's view it is precisely because the Labour left provides this link between the Labour leadership and the working class that its effect is to inhibit the militant potential of the working class. The belief that it is possible to work for socialism in and through the Labour Party is not just an illusion. It is also dangerous, because the activities of the Labour left actually serve to strengthen the ideological hold of capital. The history of Labour is not, then, that of a socialist party led astray. Rather it is a history of the use of its socialist appeal to serve its continued functioning in the interests of capital. Hence Panitch's remark that what socialist commentators see 'as Labour's failures are really its successes' (Panitch, 1976, p.235).

Now, there are many problems with this kind of argument, but what should be noted here is that it turns on the idea that the 'interests' of the working class are identifiable independently either of the activities of parties and other organizations, or of whether significant sections of the working class recognize them as such. In effect, the interests of the working class are given in the capitalist structure of the economy, and they find expression in industrial militancy and, at least potentially, in socialist politics. Periodic outbreaks of industrial militancy can then be invoked as a sign of what is still to come, demonstrating yet again that there really is a fundamental conflict of interest between the working class and the capitalist system. On the other hand, the givenness of the popular majority for socialism allows a cavalier attitude towards evidence that there is precious little working-class support for left positions. The beauty of what is given but unrealized is that it can always be invoked as a *potential* requiring only the right conditions for it to be made massively present. Thus David Coates acknowledges that the policies of the last Labour government aimed at holding down real wages failed to generate sustained working-class militancy. The problem, it seems, is not simply one of leadership incorporation, but also that of 'an entire class's cultural subordination, a passive if reluctant integration into capitalism's ruling ideology of necessity' (Coates, 1980, p.211). But all is not entirely lost, for:

> The fit between working class experience and the ruling culture is never total. There is always a 'space' which the left has got to reach, an autonomous working class subculture of mutualism and democracy which the left has got to tap ... beneath the surface of industrial peace and the 'consensus' tapped by opinion surveys lie these untapped and ill-articulated resentments ... It is these resentments which the existing parties cannot resolve (ibid. pp.272-3).

Whatever the appearances, the low level of militancy or the evidence of working-class hostility to left policies, we know that the real working-class is out there somewhere, patiently awaiting the socialist call.

## Consequences for political analysis

Now, what must be noted here is that the diverse LLG positions and their Milibandish critiques all depend on the view that there is 'a political majority inherent in Britain's social structure' (*BRS*, p.34) if only the right kind of socialist ideas could be found to realize it. The majority is already there in British society, but it has to be brought to life by the political work of socialists. The diversity of strategies derived from this position indicates that the conception of a working-class potential for socialism and of the unity-in-disunity of the left are unavoidably incomplete as means of political analysis. These conceptions do have significant consequences for political analysis, as we shall see, but the idea that there is a political majority out there waiting for the call provides only limited guidance as to how to deal with the multiplicity of interests, parties, factions, organizations and struggles currently occupying the political stage. Additional means of political assessment must therefore be employed in the tactical manoeuvrings of factions and organizations on the left, their attempted alliances, interventions, debates and internecine quarrels. It is largely at this level that the diverse LLG positions differ from each other and from their Milibandish critiques.

But although they can appear in a variety of divergent analyses and political prognoses, it would be a mistake to dismiss these general conceptions as mere rhetorical markers having no real significance when it comes to practical decision on strategy or tactics. On the contrary, they have extremely damaging effects on forms of political calculation widely employed on the left. In the following discussion I concentrate first on the idea of democracy and accountability as they appear in LLG positions and their effects on the analysis of party structure and organization and the discussion of policy within the party, and second on the effects of the idea of left unity and an inherent socialist majority. The consequences of rejecting these conceptions of socialist political analysis are considered in the following chapters.

*Democracy and accountability*
We have seen that a tendentious history of the Labour Party

as an everyday story of leadership betrayal has the effect of appearing to establish a direct link between democracy and accountability within the party and its pursuit of socialist policies. The party is essentially socialist but the leadership is in constant danger of incorporation into the *status quo*. The danger arises because of the independence of the PLP and its leadership from the rest of the movement. It is to be overcome by democratization, by making individual MPs and the PLP accountable – that is, by tying them down through reselection, NEC control of the manifesto and new procedures for appointing the party leadership. This link between democracy and socialist policies clearly depends on a particular conception of the essential socialism of the rank-and-file. Because of that essential socialism it is possible to know in advance what kinds of policies would emerge from informed discussion within the Labour Party. It is for this reason that the Labour Coordinating Committee and many other advocates of democratization can identify the campaign for party democracy with their campaigns for specific policy positions, as if failure to support the latter were itself a denial of democracy. In effect, for this conception, policy positions appear not so much as the products of discussion and investigation, but rather as expressions of the essential character of the movement. For all the need to strengthen and inform debate there is little wrong with the socialist policies that the present system of policy debate produces. Thus, echoing a well-worn tune in Labour left discussion, Frank Allaun argues in *Labour Activist* (No. 5, July 1979) that 'slight updating' apart the Labour Party has no need to develop new policies:

> We have a fine programme which has not been carried out. Our job now is to find a way of so democratizing the Labour movement that the parliamentary leaders will implement it.

Here the significance of democratizing the Labour Party is absolutely clear. Its function is not so much to transform the conditions in which policy questions are debated within the party, and possibly thereby to affect the policy positions that emerge, but rather to strengthen support for existing Labour Party policy against the party leadership.

The link between party democracy and the pursuit of socialist policies is far less certain than many on the Labour left suppose. A naive faith in the essential socialism of the party is certainly one of the problems of the LLG strategies. But the difficulties with their arguments on democracy and accountability go much further. I have argued in chapter 2 that procedures of decision-making and appointment cannot in general be subjected to a simple one-dimensional ranking, as just more democratic or less. The Labour Party arguments over procedures for reselection of MPs are an excellent illustration. The Campaign for Labour Victory argued that all members of the constituency party should be involved in the decision, while many of their opponents on the left of the party wanted it to be made by the General Management Committee (GMC). Both sides, of course, argued in the name of democracy, and in its name they advocated radically different procedures. What their debates bring out is not that one side is more committed to democracy than the other, but rather that when it comes down to the assessment of specific procedures the argument cannot proceed in terms of democracy alone. It always involves reference to other considerations; both sides in this case assuming that the GMC is likely to be to the left of the constituency membership as a whole. I have argued that 'democratic' procedures should be analysed in terms of their scope and how that scope is determined, the way they are organized and the other conditions in which they operate, and in terms of the constraints on discussion and voting, limitations of scope, and so on, which those conditions and organizational features impose. What the consequences of 'democratic' procedures are always depends on conditions not given in the scope and organization of the procedures themselves, they are never consequences of 'democracy' pure and simple. As the example of reselection shows different procedures may well have differential consequences of great importance for the various social forces concerned.

Now, it is clear that these points are frequently recognized on the left as far as severely practical matters of tactical manoeuvring are concerned. The skill with which the Campaign for Labour Party Democracy conducted its long drawn out campaign for reselection and other changes is a case in point. But the arguments for democracy and accountability in the party are nevertheless often conducted in an entirely different register, as if a simple ranking of procedures as more or less democratic were indeed possible and desirable. That simplistic position has an undeniable polemical appeal, but it also has seriously damaging consequences for political analysis, not least because once 'democratic' procedures have been identified it allows all other interventions to be represented as presumptively illegitimate. To say that democratic procedures have some definite scope is to say that they have definite limitations, in the sense that there will always be matters of interest to the relevant constituencies falling outside that scope. What those limitations are may vary, but the fact of there being some definite limitations is inescapable. To say, in the case of the Labour Party, that its 'democratic' procedures of policy formation have a particular scope is to say that many decisions relating to policy will also involve procedures which are not democratic. But it is not to say that those procedures are necessarily illegitimate or antidemocratic. Such implications are simply swept aside in many left arguments about the need for democracy and accountability within the party with damaging consequences for their analysis. Only a few of these consequences can be considered here and, by way of illustration, I shall comment briefly on the analysis of the party's organizational structure and on the discussion of policy, as these appear within LLG strategies.

Notice first that the call for democratization as a way of controlling the party leadership involves a recognition that decisions taken by conference are not the primary determinants of what the leadership does. Throughout the 1970s, the left dominated the National Executive Council and its major subcommittees, and it won support in the constituencies and trade union branches for what it believed to be good socialist policies, as represented, for example, in *Labour's Programme, 1973* and *Labour's Programme, 1976*. Throughout the decade the left fought and won many battles over party policy, but these victories were not sufficient to determine the policies of Labour governments or even the contents of the 1979 election manifesto. It is that realization more than anything else that generated the furore over democratizing the party. The problem as seen by the Labour left is clearly stated in Frank Allaun's lament quoted earlier. 'We have a fine programme which has not been carried out' (*Labour Activist*, No. 5, 1979). If that is indeed the problem, why should democracy be seen as the means of overcoming it? The invocation of democracy in this context is a recognition that there are effective sources of leadership autonomy from Conference decision: it stigmatizes them as anti-democratic and calls on Conference to vote them out of existence.

To say that there are effective sources of leadership autonomy from Conference decisions is not to say that the leadership are free of all constraint or that Conference decisions have no political effect. Conference decisions may well embarrass the party leadership, they may foster an image of the party as fractious and disunited, they may encourage Labour movement activists in their disenchantment with Labour government policies and their practical opposition to them, and they may encourage some on the left and many others on the right of the party in their pursuit of a fundamental re-alignment in British politics – and they may sometimes encourage the leadership to modify its policies. That Conference decisions are not a matter of indifference to the party leadership is evidenced in attempts to stage-manage Conference proceedings and to avoid defeats whenever possible – and, of course, in Gaitskell's massively successful campaign to reverse a Conference decision on unilateralism. But Conference decisions do not have the effect of determining the objectives pursued by the PLP or its leadership.

Sources of leadership autonomy from Conference decisions are not hard to find. Nor is it difficult to identify other significant determinants of the policies of the party leadership. For example: the leadership has to be able to carry the PLP with it on most important policy issues and it has considerable resources, of patronage on the one hand and of loyalty to the party as an electoral machine concerned with gaining power on the other, which help it to do so; the leadership have to develop some kinds of working relationships with the TUC and the leaders of the major unions, so that union voting behaviour at Conference does not represent the only or even the most important link between the party and the unions; on specific items of policy what the party has to offer is often little but more or less sophisticated propaganda masquerading as a set of policy proposals and, when Labour is in office, that 'policy' has to compete with advice from pressure groups and issue organizations and from an experienced, not always unsympathetic, civil service – and there are many in the PLP and elsewhere in the party who have little time for the predominantly expressive stance of the left on so many issues.

These points have been listed only by way of illustration, and they are certainly not intended to be exhaustive. They are, however, more than sufficient to show that the sources of leadership autonomy cannot be expected to melt away merely because Conference invites them to do so. But they also show how dangerously simplistic it is to see any deviation from policy laid down by Conference as *prima facie* evidence of leadership betrayal, something to be remedied by stricter democratic accountability. The left's everyday story of leadership betrayal is admirably suited to castigating the party leaders, but it is of limited value as political analysis since it glosses over the complexity of Labour Party organization and its diverse relations with other elements in the Labour movement, the various apparatuses of government, and numerous non-governmental organizations. There are centres of power and influence in the Labour movement and elsewhere which must be taken into account by any party leadership and which cannot be voted out of existence by however large a Conference majority – and by no means all of their interventions can seriously be regarded as illegitimate or undemocratic. Similar points apply to the position of individual MPs, Labour local authorities and individual councillors. To the extent that it has succeeded in winning support in constituency parties, union branches and Conference itself the left has also demonstrated how little such victories contribute to producing the kind of PLP and party leadership required for its dreams of a LLG. The Labour left has failed to take seriously the determinants of the policies pursued by the PLP and its leadership, or, as we shall see in a moment, the problems involved in putting policy into effect and the conditions necessary for its successful implementation. Substantial changes in the political objectives pursued by the PLP may well be achievable, and democratic reforms may well play a part in that, but it will require a constructive politics of persuasion and alliance starting from the present political concerns and objectives of the various sections of the PLP and of those in the unions, civil service and elsewhere who play a significant role in forming the policies of the parliamentary leadership.

*Policy*
I have suggested that the connection in LLG strategies between democracy and accountability within the party and its pursuit of socialist policies depends on a particular conception of the essential socialism of the rank-and-file. This last allows policy positions to appear not so much as products of investigation and informed debate but rather as expressing that essential socialism. There is an obvious tension between

this conception of policy as expression and the idea of policy as something to be considered in terms of its possible effects and the conditions required for its successful implementation. The first plays a prominent role in LLG strategies and, in extreme cases, affirmation of the expressive function of policy may even be combined with the open recognition that the policy in question may be impracticable or ineffective. We have seen an example of this in Hodgson's assessment of the AES. Unfortunately, refusal to take seriously the conditions and effects of policy implementation is by no means restricted to fringe organizations on the Labour left. There has been a widespread failure in the British Labour movement to work through the practical questions arising from the adoption of particular policy objectives or instruments. Consider the example of planning agreements, adopted with significant union support in *Labour's Programme, 1973*, ritually reaffirmed ever since and supported by the TUC. Planning agreements were to be tripartite agreements involving government, enterprise management and unions representing the workforce. They were to cover such matters as enterprise investment and employment policy, product development, etc. For planning agreements to be effective would therefore have required both unions and government to develop a capacity to negotiate with management over these matters and to monitor the implementation of agreements. But there has been little sign of any attempt to work out what consequential changes would be required in union organization or the machinery of government. The Wilson governments of the 1970s did not take the idea of planning agreements seriously, but neither did the major unions that voted for them at Conference.

This conception of policy as expressive is reflected in the manifest lack of concern in left Labour discussions of policy with the conditions in which policy issues are discussed and debated within the Labour Party. In spite of general affirmation of the need for informed debate we find little or no consideration either of the conditions in which debate presently takes place within the Labour Party and of what conditions would be required for that debate to be seriously informed about the issues. Informed debate requires informed participants. Informed debate within the Labour Party therefore presupposes forms of policy discussion whose main objective is precisely to develop an informed membership, by providing background materials and clarifying the issues, problems and difficulties involved in particular policy areas, by considering the arguments for and against alternative policy proposals and their likely consequences, and so on. But in Labour Party branches policy issues are generally discussed either in relation to resolutions, about which most members present have little or no notice and are unavoidably ill-prepared, or in the context of short, one-off discussions led by an outside speaker. In neither case are the conditions for serious and thorough consideration of the relevant issues normally present. Thus support for policy positions within the party, as seen for example in resolutions submitted to Conference, can hardly be regarded as the product of informed debate and serious reflection.

The problem of policy formulation therefore appears not so much as concerning the conditions in which policy issues are discussed, but rather as to do with the connection between the expressive moment of policy formation in the party and the actions of the parliamentary leadership. Two issues are frequently raised in left Labour discussions of this connection. First, it is suggested that Conference has sometimes been 'managed' so as to prevent the true expression of the movement from emerging. For example, 'Can we make conference more democratic?' in *Labour Activist* (No. 7, the 1979 Conference issue) points out that the Conference Arrangements Committee has 'wide powers to exclude resolutions without the party being able to see the expression of opinion contained within them', and that those powers were sometimes abused, 'for example, to keep public ownership off the agenda in the 1950's and 1960's'. Furthermore: 'Clever manipulation of the way subjects are classified can obscure *the will of the CLP's, unions and other affiliated organisations'* (emphasis added). There is obviously room for reform in the organization of Conference and there can be no denying that Conference agendas have been open to manipulation. That point is amply documented in Lewis Minkin's *The Labour Party Conference*. But what should be noted here is the terms in which *Labour Activist* makes its point. The possibility of manipulation is used not to question the notion of policy as expression, but rather to show that Conference decisions may not always properly express the will of the movement, hence the comment on public ownership just quoted. The effect is merely to shift the expression of that will one stage further back, to the resolutions submitted to Conference by CLPs, unions and other affiliated organizations. The notion that the will of the movement finds expression in those resolutions can be retained only at the cost of flagrant inconsistency. It requires reference to the conditions under which decisions are taken in order to discredit Conference as a properly democratic forum and a refusal to consider conditions of discussion in party branches in order to privilege them.

The second issue that usually arises in left discussion of policy formulation is that of implementation. It is all very well getting Conference to adopt good socialist policies but that won't get us very far if Labour governments refuse to act on them. This point has been forcefully brought home to the Labour left by the undisguised contempt of the Wilson and Callaghan governments for the economic policies contained in *Labour's Programme, 1973* and *Labour's Programme, 1976*. In this context the problem of implementation is seen as one of how to get a Labour government to take on board policies that have been determined elsewhere (i.e. by Conference) and then of how to overcome civil service opposition.

This manner of posing the question of policy implementation raises a number of issues. One has been noted above, namely the widespread lack of concern on the left with working out details of how policy is to be put into effect and what consequential changes might be needed in the organization of government, unions, and other bodies, with the obstacles that would have to be overcome and the sources of effective resistance, and so on. I have already referred to attitudes towards planning agreements as an example. For a rather different example of this lack of attention consider the statement *Banking and Finance* presented by the NEC to the 1976 Conference. Here much of the argument for bringing the major banks and insurance companies into public ownership is conducted in terms of the enormous financial power of these institutions and their failure to use that power to support the development of the national economy.

> A major extension of public ownership in these fields could facilitate a significant improvement in service to customers, ... It would also provide the instruments the British economy needs for ensuring that the financial and industrial systems operate in harmony, jointly promoting the communal interest by ensuring that savers' funds go to support the industrial investment on which jobs and real incomes depend in the long-term, instead of being siphoned off into speculative property ventures and the like (*Banking and Finance*, p.20).

Fine sentiments. But neither the document, nor subsequent Labour Party publications, pay the least attention to the question of what changes in the practices and organization of these institutions, in the relevant government departments and in the industrial enterprises that would be required to take up the necessary investment, would be needed for the pursuit of these desirable objectives. Notice also how the second of these objectives depends on conditions not within the direct control of government, in this case the behaviour of private industrial enterprises. Similar points would apply to incomes policies, statutory or voluntary, and in many other policy areas. Too often policy discussion in the Labour Party, and not just on the left, is characterized by an abject failure to consider the political and economic conditions necessary for the successful implementation of particular policies.

A final issue concerns the point at which policy is to be elaborated. What is at stake in this question depends on whether policy is considered primarily in terms of its supposed expressive function or in terms of its possible consequences and the conditions required for it to be effective. If policy is regarded as expression of the will of the movement then it seems reasonable that policy should be determined by a body that could be regarded as expressing that will, that is, by Conference, suitably modified to avoid the manipulative distortions noted above, and, between Conferences, by the NEC. Policy, in this sense, is to be determined by one body and put into effect by another – and it is that disjunction that gives rise to the peculiar form that the problem of implementation takes in so many Labour Party discussions where it is seen to be a matter of how to tie the hands of the parliamentary leadership. If, on the other hand, policy is considered in terms of its consequences and effectiveness with regard to its stated objectives then the question appears in a very different light. From this point of view it is plainly absurd for government policy to be determined by a body that carries no responsibility for putting it into effect. Indeed, given the well-known right-wing contempt for left approaches to policy issues it is tempting to suggest that its predominantly expressive conception of policy has been one of the major obstacles to the success of left positions inside the Labour Party.

There are, of course, very good reasons why the Labour Party and other organizations should conduct serious investigations into a variety of policy areas : to acquire a familiarity with the problems and constraints that policy would have to confront, a knowledge of the range of policy options available and their likely costs and consequences, to build up teams of specialist advisers so that incoming Labour ministers would not be wholly at the mercy of their civil servants, and so on. But the objectives of such investigations would not be so much to determine what the policies of a Labour government should be – for the particular conditions and constraints within which governments will have to act cannot be determined in advance, and there will always be areas where policy cannot be worked out in any detail outside the relevant government department. The point rather would be to provide greater knowledge and back-up facilities so as to improve the conditions in which Labour governments or ministers within them can act in pursuit of their objectives, and the conditions in which backbench MPs and others can seriously question the performance of ministers and government departments.

The problem confronting the Labour left is not that the Labour Party has perfectly good policies that Labour governments have stubbornly refused to implement. Whatever may be thought of the quality of those policies, it would be a dangerous oversimplification to suppose that government policies either can or should be laid down by outside bodies independently of the specific constraints facing governments given the conditions in which they have no choice but to act.

*Left unity and the inherent majority for socialism*
We have seen that the notions of the unity-or-disunity of the left and of the inherent but unrealized majority for socialism in British society perform two significant roles in LLG strategies. On the one hand mass struggle outside parliament is often said to have a vital role to play in socialist politics. I return to that issue in a moment. On the other hand the notions of left unity and inherent majority appear to provide socialist political analysis with a given that has yet to be constructed, that is they serve to identify what, in spite of manifest differences, have to be brought together. I have argued that the notion of an inherent socialist majority depends on a highly problematic conception of 'interests' as given essentially in the structure of the economy and existing

quite independently either of the political work of parties, the media and other agencies or of the manifest political concerns and objectives of the members of that 'majority'. What should be noted here is the way that the given but unrealized character of the unity and popular majority generates a number of significant political demarcations. If there is an inherent majority then there is no need to look beyond its boundaries for the makings of an effective majority. In that sense it defines the boundaries of the unity that is to be constructed, thereby drawing the line against opponents of the left, the Tories, right-wing Labour MPs and leaderships that adopt Tory policies, etc. This boundary effectively circumscribes the field of potential allies, thus allowing many of the Labour left to oppose alliance with the Liberals towards the end of the Callaghan government and even to welcome defections from Labour to SDP. Sometimes a further boundary to the unity may be set to cut out the non-democratic or insurrectionary left, so that what has to be united are those on the left prepared to operate within and by means of the institutions of parliamentary democratic politics.

But, there are also differences even within what, on this conception, has to be united, and these are thought to function as an obstacle to the achievement of unity. For example, the differences between the Lucas Aerospace combine and the left-wing leadership of TASS; between the CPGB and all those other groups and organizations on the left who stubbornly refuse to fall in line behind the leadership it pretends to offer; differences within the union movement and between unions and women's organizations over discriminatory employment practices and priorities in collective bargaining. As these examples suggest, the abstractly defined unity of the left covers a multitude of substantive differences between its supposed component parts in terms of their political concerns and objectives, the kinds of changes they aim at, the obstacles they confront and the conditions they have to work on.

Now, it is clear that left unity cannot be dismissed simply as a figment of left imagination. Distinct left groups have sometimes come together to form real and effective unities, for example, in the AUEW and the NUS and, in the later stages of the campaign for 'democratic' reforms and the first deputy leadership contest, the Rank-and-File Mobilizing Committee in the Labour Party. There are also a number of unifying themes, such as anti-racism or defence of union rights, that allow diverse positions to come together for limited action in common. But what is proposed in the LLG strategies goes far beyond those limited and more or less effective forms of unity. It is nothing less than a national unity of the left operating at a variety of levels, including that of parliamentary and electoral politics. At that level differences of the kind noted above pose a real problem for exponents of LLG strategies. They cannot be wished away by vague talk of an underlying unity of purpose, whether that be conceived as a unity of democratic forces, of the victims of capitalist crises, of 'all the oppressed and excluded groups in our society' (Cripps *et al*, 1981, p.18), or whatever. Talk of unity does not suffice to unify the diverse forces of the left. We have already noted the tendency of LLG strategies to discount both current political concerns and objectives, except perhaps as a means of gathering support, and the problems of achieving particular policy objectives. The real and often severe differences within the left over political concerns and objectives are thereby discounted in the name of an altogether grander unity, whose very lack of definition allows those who talk of left unity to compete for each other's supporters by pretending to offer the politics around which the unity of the left might finally be constructed.

The assumptions of unity and an inherent socialist majority therefore have significant disabling effects. First, they allow the possibility of significant alliances with non-socialist elements to be dismissed without argument as irrelevant, given the built-in though latent support for socialism. Second, they obscure the fact that differences between components of that supposed socialist majority may be as severe in many cases as those imagined to exist between socialist and non-socialist. Third, they inhibit serious consideration of possible areas of alliance around seriously negotiated objectives. An important example under present conditions would be an alliance against Thatcherism, which might include some Conservatives, but would certainly involve serious participation by Liberals and the SDP as well as the Labour right and centre.

Finally, if the ideas of left unity and inherent majority for socialism are highly problematic, what of the role often assigned to mass, extra-parliamentary politics in LLG strategies. The importance of popular struggles in British political history, to say nothing of other societies, is undeniable, and we have seen that an important part of the CPGB argument for extra-parliamentary struggle is that 'major changes won throughout the history of the labour movement have come mainly as a result of struggle outside Parliament' (*BRS*, p.35). That may be, but it is far from clear what relevance such invocation has to the analysis of contemporary conditions. Socialists in Britain today are not confronted with the political conditions of the past: when limited adult suffrage restricted the possibility of political participation through electoral channels and before the rise of mass membership parties and the development of the major unions and the TUC into significant political actors that any government (even the present one) must take note of or suffer the consequences, before the development of modern techniques of political campaigning through opinion sampling and the media, and so on. Tales of how changes were won then are not a reliable guide to how they may be won now, and socialists can ill afford to rely on the benefit of hindsight in their present struggles. This invocation of history is a way of refusing to come to terms with the conditions confronting socialist politics today. The point here is not at all to say that non-parliamentary movements have no role to play in socialist politics: quite the contrary, and I have argued above for the importance of developing non-parliamentary forms of popular control over the practices of the state apparatuses. The point rather is that assessment of the possible role of extra-parliamentary struggle in obtaining changes through parliament should be a matter not of romantic nostalgia but of careful analysis of contemporary political conditions.

# 4 Problems of political support

In the last chapter I discussed some of the general conceptions of socialist politics to be found on the Labour left, and to some extent elsewhere, in which the primary objective of socialist strategic calculation is supposed to be the achievement of a left Labour government An influential critique of that objective is based on closely related conceptions of socialist politics. These general conceptions concern the unity-in-disunity of the left and the mass base for socialist politics that is supposed to be inherent in British society, and they involve a tendentious history of the Labour Party as a cautionary tale of leadership betrayal and a predominantly expressive orientation towards questions of policy. These themes are brought together into 'strategies' for achieving a left Labour government: the left is to be united around policies capable of mobilizing the potential electoral support for socialism that is supposed to be already present in British society. The aim is to bring about the major societal change described in *Labour's Programme, 1973* as involving 'a fundamental and irreversible shift in the balance of power and wealth', and it is suggested that nothing less than such a change would be capable of resolving the social and economic problems of contemporary Britain. These strategies for a left Labour government play a major part in left-wing political discussion, although they by no means exhaust political calculation on the left. I have argued that the principal elements of these strategies and the ways in which they constrain political calculation and the definition of socialist objectives must play a large part in the explanation of the widespread failure of the left to seriously consider policy in terms of what would be involved in putting it into effect and the political and economic conditions necessary for its successful implementation, and of the equally widespread failure to come to terms with the problems of winning support for their policies within the Labour movement and especially within the electorate.

This chapter considers the consequences of rejecting the general conceptions of socialist politics particularly associated with these strategies. An obvious consequence is that if there is no general problem of the unity of 'the left' or 'the movement' and there is no pre-given majority for socialism in British social structure just waiting to be realized, then socialist politics cannot be subordinated to the one primary objective of the realization of that unity and that majority. Dissolution of that problem of unity poses instead the problems of constructing political support for particular sets of objectives, problems concerning alliances rather than the realization of some pre-given unity. To insist on left unity is to discount the political effects of manifest and often bitter disagreements over political objectives and more general principles to be found on the left.

I have already referred to the example of the Lucas Aerospace combine who confronted a major obstacle that their methods and objectives were incompatible with the commitment to centralized control that characterizes the 'left-wing' leadership of TASS. To talk of unity in this context is to discount those differences, to treat the specific objectives of the Lucas combine as insignificant compared with the underlying commonality of interests which is supposed to unite them with some of their most implacable opponents. Or again, we might consider the tensions between socialist feminism and other positions on the left: for example, in relation to the negotiating stance of all too many unions over sex discrimination, or the prioritization of pay over other questions of hours and working conditions, or in relation to the politics of the family of the CPAG. To discount those differences in favour of some underlying unity of the working class and its allies is effectively to trivialize the specific objectives of socialist feminism. There is no shortage of other examples. To talk of unity in the face of such differences is to discount the specific objectives and principles around which groups organize and about which they differ. But to recognize those differences and to take them seriously is to say that there is no common problem of strategy for the left as such and in general. It is to pose problems of strategy rather at the level of specifiable objectives and the available means and conditions of working towards them. Many of those objectives will differ from one group or organization to another, giving rise to significant disputes on the left that cannot be resolved except by transforming the practices or objectives of at least one of the disputing parties. Some objectives depend on legislation and some require transformations at other levels, for example, changes in the negotiating stance of unions on issues affecting the conditions of employment of women or in the organizational practices of TASS.

But the dependence of some objectives on legislation raises the issue of parliamentary and electoral majorities, and this will be my main concern in this chapter. Now there is a sense in which the strategies for a left Labour government do recognize the importance of constructing parliamentary majorities. They aim to create a Labour Party committed to a programme of socialist transformation of British society as a true expression of the interests of the Labour movement and, did they but know it, of the vast majority of the British public. I have argued that these strategies involve an expressive conception of policy, a failure to consider the conditions of policy discussion inside the Labour Party and the unions or the political and economic conditions needed for the successful implementation of particular policy proposals, and an inability to come to terms with major centres of power and influence inside the Labour movement. To reject the conceptual foundations of these strategies is to pose the problems of constructing effective support for legislation or executive action in the context of a non-expressive commitment to policy objectives. Some of these can no doubt be dealt with through pressure group politics or private members bills, but in general there are severe problems in getting parliamentary support or time on issues that do not form part of the parliamentary programme of a major party.

So, although the expressive and programmatic Labour Party of the left Labour government strategies may be a romantic illusion, socialists (or anyone else) concerned with social and economic reform, with running central and local government, with managing the economy and establishing greater public control over its functioning, are still confronted with the necessity of working through the construction of electoral and parliamentary majorities. My point here is not that socialism can be achieved 'through the ballot box alone' (Hain, 1981, p.188) but simply that precious little will be achieved without it. To say that without invoking the pie in the sky of an electoral majority patiently awaiting the socialist call is to say that policy objectives and programmes have to be considered in terms of the problems of getting effective support in the labour movement and elsewhere from existing centres of power and bases of political organization, and of obtaining significant parliamentary and electoral support starting from present political conditions in Britain. This will involve working with some of those in the labour movement whose socialism is not that of the left, and probably with groups and organizations that would not consider themselves socialist at all. That prospect may not appeal to much of the traditional left, but failure to take seriously the problems of constructing effective political support out of existing political forces and ideologies is a guarantee of impotence.

Socialists have no alternative but to be concerned with the furthering of policy objectives through government and,

*Problems of political support*

therefore, with winning and sustaining electoral support. Current strategies of the Labour left are weak on both counts, and so, for rather different reasons, are those of the Labour right. This chapter examines left and right assessments of the relations between Labour and its actual or potential support, arguing that both are seriously deficient, and considers some of the issues involved in improving Labour's electoral position. To introduce this discussion let me begin by summarizing the evidence concerning popular support for Labour and attitudes towards its stance on policy issues.

## The secular decline in Labour support

Popular support for Labour has, with few interruptions, fallen steadily since the early 1950's. At the time of writing the success of the SDP-Liberal alliance in by-elections and its standing in opinion polls suggests that the secular decline in Labour support is in danger of becoming a catastrophic collapse. This picture of decline is least clear at the level of individual membership. Labour Party figures show a fall from over a million in 1952 to about 300,000 in 1979, but the pattern of decline is undoubtedly obscured by the operation throughout much of that period of a minimum affiliation rule of 1,000 for constituency parties. Nevertheless it is difficult to dispute Forester's claim that Labour lost more than half its individual membership between 1951 and 1970 (Forester, 1976, p.79). There is some, rather patchy, evidence of membership growth during the 1970s and there has certainly been some expansion since the 1979 election (Minkin and Seyd, 1979a).

But, whatever may have happened to individual membership, the fall in more general popular support for Labour is undeniable. With the single exception of 1966, the proportion of the electorate voting Labour has fallen from one General Election to the next, even during periods of Conservative government, and it has fallen considerably from 36.3 per cent in 1966 to 28 per cent in 1979. Labour was able to win elections in spite of its declining basis of electoral support because there had been a long term decline in support for the two major parties with no third party yet in a position to challenge their electoral dominance. The two-party share of the electorate fell from 77.5 per cent in 1951 to 54.6 per cent in October, 1974 rising again to 63.2 per cent with the Conservative success in 1979. Support for the SDP-liberal alliance in by-elections and opinion polls suggests a real possibility that the period of two-party electoral dominance has come to an end.

Voting studies indicate that party allegiances within the electorate and their association with class were getting weaker throughout the 1960s and subsequently. The authors of *Political Change in Britain* suggest that the image of politics in terms of conflicting class interests was most widely accepted amongst those who entered the electorate during and immediately after the Second World War, and that it had significantly less appeal amongst younger Labour supporters. Their results also show a declining association throughout the 1960s between class and party in all age groups. The Essex studies, based on post-election surveys covering elections from 1964 to October 1974, indicate that both the proportion of the electorate not voting on class lines and the proportion not committed to one or other major party were substantial and growing. In particular they note a 'fall in support for Labour Party principles amongst its own identifiers – in particular, its younger, working class and trade unionist core' (Crewe *et al*, 1977, p.198). The polls show that while Labour's middle-class support held up reasonably well between 1974 and 1979, there was a fall in working-class support, especially during the 1978–9 winter of discontent, and among skilled workers in particular (Mitchell, 1979; Kellner, 1979). This is not to say, of course, that Labour has suffered an irreversible loss of working-class support, or that it cannot win another election.

*Problems of political support*

But there has been a marked decline in identification with Labour as the party of the working class, and a weakening of voter-identification with either Labour or Conservative leading to a growing electoral volatility.

As for Labour's association with policy positions and its trade union connections, all the evidence points to a long term erosion of support. As long ago as 1960 Crosland could cite Gallup-poll evidence of a 'steady 20-year decrease in the numbers of those who think the unions a good thing' (Crosland, 1960, p.9), and he then went on to argue that Labour's identification with the unions was coming to be an electoral liability. Unions have hardly become more popular in the subsequent period. *Political Change in Britain* noted in the 1960s a growing proportion of the electorate who felt that the unions had too much power, and a MORI poll in 1980 showed a clear majority of union members sharing that view (*Sunday Times*, 31 August 1980). There is little new either in the lack of support for Labour policy positions, even amongst Labour voters. In *Must Labour Lose?* Mark Abrams reported a drastic change in attitudes towards public ownership amongst Labour supporters. 'In 1949, 60 per cent were in favour of extending public ownership; in 1960 58 per cent were opposed' (Abrams *et al* p.37). More recently, the Essex studies noted a growth in diffuse dissatisfaction with their party's policies over the period 1964-74 amongst both Labour and Conservative supporters. They also show, amongst Labour's working-class supporters, a growing disaffection from Labour's established policy positions on public expenditure on social security and social services generally, on public ownership and on racial integration.

In short, there were declining trends in popular support for Labour operating well before the formation of the SDP and its alliance with the Liberals in 1981. What had seemed in the late 1940s and 1950s to be a firm connection between class and party identification no longer holds. Labour has lost support for its policy positions within the working class, its own supporters are less likely to interpret their partisanship in class terms, and there has been a steady decline in its electoral support.

## What went wrong?

These facts are well known, and they should seriously disturb anyone concerned with furthering socialist objectives through legislation and government action. The point was forcefully made over twenty years ago by Anthony Crosland in his Fabian pamphlet, *Can Labour Win?* After a preliminary listing of socialist principles, few of which would now be disputed by the Labour left, he goes on to suggest that 'socialists who read this pamphlet are interested in realizing these aims in practice: that is, they are concerned with political achievement' (Crosland, 1960, p.2). Since in his view that achievement would depend on electing a Labour government and sustaining it in office, he insists on the need to investigate political attitudes and voting behaviour, arguing that consideration of these matters should be based on 'information rather than on whim or hunch' (ibid., p.3). Crosland's pamphlet epitomizes an influential approach to the problem of Labour's electoral support, and I will return to his arguments in a moment.

But first, consider how the evidence of declining Labour support appears from the perspective of the left Labour government strategies and related conceptions of socialist politics. If there is a potential socialist majority inherent in Britain's social structure, how is Labour's poor showing to be explained? We have seen that the inherent majority is supposed to consist primarily of the working class, supplemented by other groups oppressed by modern society. The working class has distinctive political and economic interests to which Labour with its union connections and socialist rhetoric, appeals but fails to adequately represent. Starting from the premise of an inherent socialist majority the failure of Labour to realize that majority may be assessed in one of two ways. On the one hand there is the argument of Miliband and others that Labour is not and cannot become an effective force for socialism. From that perspective its union connections and the rhetoric of the Labour left actually serve the interests of capital by attracting working-class support for Labour, thereby containing its inherent socialism. The left Labour government strategies interpret Labour's history rather differently. Labour has indeed failed to realize its true potential support in the country, and in the working class in particular. The reason, as *Manifesto* puts it, is that 'part of the movement, especially its official representatives and leaders, abandoned a class-based socialist strategy in favour of a compromise with the existing structures of power' (Cripps *et al*, 1981, p.105).

In effect, the story is that Labour at once appeals to and suppresses a distinctive working-class politics, and its persistent failure to deliver on its socialist promise undermines its hold over working-class loyalties. Thus *Manifesto* acknowledges the long term loss of votes and decline in support for Labour's policies, and attributes them to the party's revisionist leadership. Revisionism blurred the party's socialist message, thereby reducing its class appeal and alienating its more committed supporters. As for the declining trend in commitment to Labour policies even amongst its own supporters, that, too, can be blamed on the revisionist leadership:

> support for nationalization among Labour sympathisers did fall between 1964 and 1970, and from 1974-9, but it had picked up noticeably up to 1974 after Labour's leadership swung behind the party's aggressive industrial policy with its emphasis on public ownership. Perhaps the unsurprising lesson really is that Labour supporters respond to what the party is telling them (Cripps *et al*, 1981, p.107-8).

Labour's decline is not the fault of the left: 'Revisionism was the cause of Labour's long term loss of vitality and support' (ibid., p.112). From this perspective the remedy is clear. It is to 'democratize' the party, thereby subjecting its wayward leadership to the party's socialist objectives and releasing its capacity to secure mass popular support.

The story is a fantasy from beginning to end, playing crucially on the most problematic conceptions of socialist political analysis identified in chapter three. We have seen that the idea of an inherent mass base for socialism depends on a highly problematic notion of political interests. The 'interests' of the working class are supposed to be inherent in the capitalist structure of the economy and they therefore exist quite independently of whether significant numbers of the working class are prepared to recognize them as such. Labour gains working-class support in so far as it appeals to those interests and loses it in so far as it betrays them or reduces that appeal. It is that conception of 'interests' that sustains the left Labour government strategies and their Milibandish critiques in the persistent disregard of the compelling evidence of working-class refusal to support the policies favoured by the Labour left, let alone the left outside the Labour Party. Or again, we have seen how the idea of the essential socialism of the Labour party is able to sustain a tendentious and misleading history of the party and a naive confusion of democratization with support for what are identified as socialist policies. The history of the party as essentially socialist has clause 4 of its constitution and other symbolic pronouncements to recommend it, but very little else. The socialist organizations that took part with the unions in the organization of the Labour Party did not do so because they thought it would be a socialist party, but rather because of their own failure as independent organizations to attract significant working-class support (Forester, 1976). Socialism, of one kind or another, has always been a significant element in the Labour Party, but it has never been the dominant element. To construct a history of the party as essentially socialist but persistently betrayed by its leaders is to invoke precisely that dubious notion of working-class interests noted above, for it requires that we discount the overwhelming and long standing evidence that there has been precious little working-class support for the 'socialist' policies of the left.

Thus the myth of the inherent socialist majority combines with a fantastic history of the Labour Party to allow many on the left to refuse the problem Crosland tries to pose. They generate disastrous consequences for the analysis of relations between Labour and its actual or potential supporters and for the 'strategies' that are supposed to follow from that analysis. The strategies for a left Labour government can acknowledge the long term decline in Labour support and yet discount it as a problem for their policies. They are complicated expressions of an act of faith in the socialist potential of the working class, rather than serious attempts to tackle the problems of advancing socialist objectives through an electorally successful Labour Party.

## Party images and discriminating voters

Now there is an alternative tradition of analysis of relations between Labour and its actual or potential supporters that appears to pride itself on taking those problems seriously. It presents us with opinion studies and electoral statistics showing that Labour is associated with several unpopular political images and that there has been a breakdown in the class alignment of electoral support. Electoral success for Labour is therefore said to depend on winning the support of that large and growing section of the electorate voting not on class lines, but in the light of party images, including assessments of the parties' performance in office.

Crosland's Fabian pamphlet, *Can Labour Win?*, published in the wake of Labour's 1959 election defeat, remains one of the best examples of this approach. Closely related arguments can also be found in Rita Hinden's rather confused analysis of 'The Lessons for Labour' in *Must Labour Lose?*, published in the same year as Crosland's pamphlet, in Austin Mitchell's Fabian Tract, *Can Labour Win Again?*, written after Labour's 1979 defeat, and in the work of many academic students of voting behaviour. Crosland argued that the declining trend in support for Labour between 1951 and 1959 resulted from two interrelated problems. First, economic development meant that the working class had become a smaller proportion of the employed population, and it produced affluence, social and geographical mobility and the destruction of old working-class communities. The working class was therefore smaller and its more prosperous sections had 'acquired a middle class income and pattern of consumption, and sometimes a middle class psychology' (Crosland, 1960, p.12). That apparent erosion of class as a basis for Labour's electoral support is what makes the role of other determinants of electoral behaviour so important in Crosland's argument. With the decline of the class alignment 'the voters may make a less automatic assessment of where their political interests lie' (ibid., p.22), and it is for that reason that he is so concerned with party images and their relation to the interests and concerns of the electorate. At that level, Crosland argued, Labour faces serious problems: the concern with full employment and the Welfare State had long since (in 1969) ceased to be identified exclusively with Labour; Labour's identification with the unions meant that it suffered from their unpopularity and that it was identified, more than the Conservatives, as a sectional or class party; and it was associated with too many unpopular images – bureaucracy, controls, nationalization, endemic splits and internal conflict.

The implications of Crosland's argument for the Labour Party are clear: it must adapt itself to the modern world or perish. In particular it must adjust to the declining importance of class as a basis for electoral support and the correlative growth in importance of party image and performance. It must break away from its identification with the working class by developing a classless appeal, and it should reduce its association with unpopular images. As Mitchell, writing some twenty years after Crosland, puts it, Labour should adopt the model of the SPD in Germany, moving 'to the middle of the road, modifying policy, toning down ideology, and becoming a much less socialist and electorally more attractive party' (Mitchell, 1979, p.11).

How is Crosland's argument, and the tradition of analysis that it represents, to be assessed? Two points should be made before proceeding. First, there is little in the development of British society over the past twenty years to significantly weaken the force of Crosland's main points. The manual working class has declined further as a proportion of the employed population and the class alignment of the electorate has now effectively collapsed. As for images, there is one respect in which things are less clear than at the time of Crosland's pamphlet. However much the performance of the 1974–9 Labour government may have disturbed Labour's association with the maintenance of full employment and the Welfare State, the present Conservative government has ensured that these are no longer non-partisan issues. In other respects the situation is as Crosland described it or worse. The popularity of the unions has not improved, Labour continues to be associated with unpopular images, and there is evidence of much reduced working-class support for public expenditure on social services and social security.

Second, the problems of electoral support Crosland tries to address cannot be discounted on the grounds of his opposition to the socialism of the Labour left. The pursuit of political objectives through legislation and government action requires that suitable governments are elected and maintained in office. If that seemed to be a serious enough problem from the mildly egalitarian and reformist standpoint of Crosland's socialism, then it should be all the more serious for those who would use the Labour Party as a vehicle for more radical transformations of our society. The problems of furthering socialist objectives through government are not peculiar to Crosland's brand of socialism and no ritual invocation of an inherent socialist majority or denunciation of Crosland and others who argue in similar vein will make them go away.

No, there are indeed problems with Crosland's argument, but it is not because the prospects for Labour have improved since 1960. If anything, they are now significantly worse. Neither is it simply a function of his distinctive brand of socialist politics. But there are nevertheless serious weaknesses both in the way he presents the argument and in the conclusions he draws. There are several issues here, but they can probably best be introduced by beginning with what Crosland describes as 'The Decline of the Working Class' (Crosland, 1960, p.10.). The argument here is that the gradual decline of the manual working class as a proportion of the employed population meant that Labour's class identification was at best a wasting asset and at worst a growing electoral liability. The relative size of the manual working class did indeed fall throughout the 1950s (by about 0.5 per cent a year) and it has continued to do so. But the implications of such changes in the occupational structure are by no means as unambiguous as Crosland suggests. It is far from clear, for example, that those moving into the expanding middle-class occupations from working-class backgrounds would be repelled by Labour's class identification (Minkin and Seyd, 1979b).

But what should be noted here is how that part of Crosland's argument depends on the presumption of a straightforward association between class and voting behaviour. Given that association it follows that a fall in the relative size of the working class entails a corresponding fall in Labour's class-based support, which Labour should try to make up for in other ways. Labour's difficulty is compounded, in Crosland's argument, by the gradual breakdown of that association. 'As economic class conflict grows less violent with the rise in living standards. . . . the voters may make a *less automatic assessment* of where their political interests lie' (Crosland, 1960, p.22, emphasis added). In similar vein Mitchell, some twenty years later, refers to the 'fading of the traditional class allegiance. . . . Those set loose from class constraints will view parties primarily in terms of their effectiveness as governments' (Mitchell, 1979, p.8). The claim is that there are two kinds of voter, those who vote 'automatically' on class lines and those who engage in some assessment of party images and their record in government, and that the second category has grown at the expense of the first.

Now, there are serious objections both to the distinction that is drawn between the two kinds of voter and to the way the supposed shift from one to the other is explained. That there has been a change within the electorate is not in dispute. In the good old days a large proportion of the working class voted Labour and, on the evidence of opinion polls and voting studies, would frequently explain that behaviour by reference to class. Over the years fewer have voted Labour and fewer still would account for doing so in class terms. What is objectionable is the way that change is represented in Crosland's argument. Reference to voters who make 'a less automatic assessment' or are 'set loose from class constraints' carries the clear implication that some more or less rational process of evaluation of the parties is engaged in by the one kind of voter, but not by the other. The pejorative character of that distinction is merely the obverse of the complacent assumption, by no means confined to the Labour left, that the working class is Labour's natural constituency. Such complacency is indefensible, and Crosland is right to attack it. His mistake is to accept much of the class reductionism of his opponents, arguing merely that the younger and more prosperous working class are beginning to escape from its influence and therefore think more carefully about how they vote. If it can be claimed that parties are assessed by the one kind of voter there is no reason to deny that they are also assessed by the other, albeit not in terms of the images Crosland would prefer Labour to project.

This point is worth stressing for it has important implications for the kind of explanation Crosland proposes. His argument is that class has become less important in determining voting behaviour as a result of secular changes in British society that are themselves largely a function of economic growth. Rather than vote 'automatically' a growing proportion of the electorate now give more thought to their voting behaviour, and that is why party images are now so important. Since that change is described as an increase in those who evaluate parties in terms of how party images and performance relate to their own concerns, it cannot be the result of their assessments of the parties' own behaviour. In effect, because of the terms in which the change is initially described, the argument has to assume that a crucial change in the political orientations of the electorate is independent of the behaviour of the parties themselves: it is given to politics by economic growth; the parties must adapt or perish.

Here Crosland reproduces an error noted in earlier chapters in connection with marxist analyses of parliamentary democracies. He treats the political concerns and orientations of the electorate as if they were formed independently of the political work of parties and other political agencies, ultimately as a function of the economy. At one time class was the main determinant of voting but, and here the echo of Bernstein is unmistakable, with the rise in living standards 'we may find.... as material pressures ease and the problem of subsistence fades away, people become more sensitive to moral and intellectual issues' (Crosland, 1960, p.22). Similarly *Political Change in Britain* presents 'the betterment of the electorate's economic conditions' as 'by far the most important of the social trends which have weakened the inclination to see politics in terms of class' (Butler and Stokes, 1974, p.193).

## Problems of political support

There is an important component of economic reductionism in these attempts to explain the decline in class alignment as a consequence of the rise in living standards and changes in occupational structure resulting from economic growth. Once again, the fact of 'affluence' is not in dispute. In today's climate talk of working-class affluence may sound somewhat hollow. But there can be little doubt that by the end of the 1950s the bulk of the working population were significantly more prosperous than at any time in the past. Even today, living standards are generally well in advance of those in the inter-war and most of the post-war periods. In that sense, however limited, 'affluence' is undeniable, but its political repercussions are another matter entirely. Crosland and other advocates of the 'affluent worker' explanation of political change have been remarkably unclear as to the mechanisms that are supposed to connect increasing prosperity with Conservative voting. Academic critics have shown that what might seem to be the most plausible mechanisms have little empirical foundation (Goldthorpe and Lockwood, 1963; Goldthorpe *et al* 1968). But even at the time of Crosland's pamphlet the 'affluent worker' thesis was not supported by the evidence. The results of the *Socialist Commentary* survey presented in the first part of *Must Labour Lose?* shows that working-class 'affluence' was not particularly associated with Conservative voting. The one index of 'affluence' that did seem to be associated with Conservative voting was house ownership. But, as Abrams suggests, it is more plausible to see that as a function of the way that house ownership had been appropriated as a political issue by the Conservatives than as a consequence of affluence as such. Even *Political Change in Britain*, after firmly embracing the 'affluent worker' thesis, then goes on to suggest that one important reason for the reduction in class polarization of the electorate during the 1960s was that 'the parties have presented the electorate with a class stimulus that is very much weaker both in terms of personnel and policy. Labour's transformation has been especially striking' (Butler and Stokes, 1974, p.195). In particular, they cite Labour's confrontations with the unions as blurring 'Labour's image as a class party' (ibid., p.198). It may be, as Minkin and Seyd (1979b) suggest, that at least part of the decline in the salience of class results from Labour's all too successful attempts to manipulate its image and electoral appeal in line with Crosland's recommendations.

## Party policy and popular concerns

The long term decline in class polarization of the electorate and the weakening of electoral support for (what used to be) the two major parties do indeed pose serious problems for Labour, and they are far more urgent today than at the time of Crosland's pamphlet. What is so problematic in the arguments of Crosland and his successors is that their account of electoral change, and the political conclusions they draw from it, involve the most simplistic conceptions of party 'images' and of voters and how they assess Labour and other parties. I have suggested that there is an important component of economic reductionism in Crosland's account of the electoral repercussions of economic growth. This is particularly striking in the argument that economic growth, of itself and independently of the practices of parties and other political agencies, brings about a kind of political *fait accompli*, in the form of a weakening of class divisions and an increase in non-class based assessments of the parties, to which the parties have no choice but to adapt.

My point here is to bring out a serious flaw in Crosland's argument, not to suggest that Labour should now try to reconstruct what remains of its class appeal. This latter view is, of course, implicit in the various left Labour government strategies with their dreams of an inherent working-class majority for socialism, but such dreams apart, there is little to be said for it. It may well be that the actions of the Labour Party and Labour governments have been in part responsible for the declining salience of class in British electoral politics. But that is not to say that those changes can now be wished away or easily reversed.

Consider, for example, *Manifesto*'s insistence that Labour can and should construct a basis of popular support extending far beyond the manual working class: 'but it must be from a class base. . . . class remains a dominant feature of British society. Class can revive as an issue which determines political loyalties' (Cripps *et al*, 1981, p.122). The existence of major social, political and economic inequalities in British society is undeniable, and they are matters of serious concern to socialists. In that sense class does indeed remain a dominant feature. But it is impossible to move directly from that point to political conclusions concerning the potential of any class-based electoral appeal under contemporary British conditions. Classes do not exist as political actors, and we have seen that arguments which ascribe a fundamental mobilizing role to class interests involve a speculative notion of interests and extremely problematic histories of the Labour Party. It is precisely that notion of interests, as existing independently of whether they are acknowledged as such, which sustains so much of the left in its flagrant disregard for the evidence concerning working-class concerns and political involvement throughout this century. In the 1950s and 1960s, many of Labour's working-class supporters may have explained their behaviour by reference to class. But it is far from clear that 'class', in the sense of that cultural and political identification, corresponds to the sense of 'class' in much Labour left or marxist argument.

The undoubted electoral significance that 'class' had for a period in British politics does not necessarily support left analyses in terms of the fundamental mobilizing role of class interests. But, however that may be, those days are now long past, and Labour is confronted with problems of electoral support under conditions in which the alleged mobilizing role of class interests certainly cannot be presumed. Crosland's point that Labour has to consider its potential electoral support and how that support might be affected by its behaviour in or out of office should now be well taken. It has been reinforced by the consequences of another important political change.

Throughout most of the post-war period British electoral competition was dominated by two major parties. Under these conditions it was possible to claim that elections were lost by the party in government, rather than won by the opposition. The implication was that within very broad limits it did not matter too much what specific policies the opposition party adopted so far as its chances of winning the next election were concerned. Remnants of such a view can still be found in the argument, advanced by Labour Solidarity and many others, that Labour should stop arguing over policy and unite to fight the Tories. Arguing over policy is divisive and it adversely affects popular support for Labour. There can be little dispute about that, at least in the short term. But the next step is more problematic: if we can stop fighting each other and stick to attacking the Tories, victory will be delivered into our hands. Until recently the complacency over policy implicit in this second step may well have been justified in terms of its short-term consequences. The danger was that short-term electoral success could mask a longer-term erosion of popular support. I argued earlier that elections should not be regarded as aggregating the wishes or opinions of the electorate, since their results depend crucially on what electoral choices are on offer. The effects of the SDP-Liberal alliance provide an excellent case in point, where the emergence of an additional electoral choice has drastically affected support for what had previously been considered the major alternatives. We have seen that the Essex studies noted an increasing disaffection from their parties' policy amongst both Labour and Conservative supporters. But that did not

## Problems of political support

put the electoral position of these two parties seriously at risk until the formation of what seemed to be a viable third alternative in the SDP-Liberal alliance. Now, whatever Labour may have got away with in the past, it cannot afford the luxury of waiting for a Conservative government to destroy itself. The emergence of the SDP-Liberal alliance means that the task of winning positive support for Labour can no longer be avoided.

The formation and apparent strength of the alliance has further important consequences which I will return to below. For the moment, consider the question of how Labour might adapt to the unpopularity of many of its major policy positions, or to the electoral problems posed by its links with the unions. Should Labour abandon its unpopular policy positions? Should it merely play them down at election time? Or should it attempt to modify popular perceptions of what it regards as central policy issues? Evidence concerning Labour's image and the popularity or otherwise of some of its policy positions cannot determine which of these responses should be chosen. Both the first and the third response have found respectable support within the party. The first appears most clearly in revisionists' impatience with the Labour left, especially in their critique of the left's obsession with nationalization, and in Mitchell's argument that Labour should be less ideological, 'becoming a much less socialist and electionally more attractive party' (Mitchell, 1979, p.11). There may well be something to be said for this argument, but Crosland, and especially his successors (eg, Mitchell, 1979; Leonard, 1981) are sometimes too ready to move directly from the evidence of the polls to conclusions regarding party policy and organization – as if the primary function of that evidence is to provide yet another weapon against the left, thereby clearing the ground for whatever policies or party reforms they might wish to advocate.

In other contexts, where issues not particularly associated with the left are concerned, the third response comes to the fore. Crosland argues that the party must create a new image by adopting a clear set of priorities.

> What is required is to select a limited number of vital issues, stemming from the basic socialist principles summarised earlier, and to propagate these insistently and purposefully for the whole period between now and the next election (Crosland, 1960, p.18).

Crosland's 1960 list of priorities need not concern us here. What should be noted is the clear recognition at this point of his argument that electoral attitudes are not political givens, products of an underlying social and economic structure, that they are not independent of the practices of parties and other political actors. There can be no reason then for supporting policies merely because they are popular with the voters or for jettisoning others because they are not. If electoral unpopularity is to be used against policies of public ownership favoured by the left, then Croslandite egalitarianism and commitment to a high level of public spending would fare little better.

Such unprincipled opportunism apart, there can be no easy answers to the question of how Labour should take account of the current concerns of voters and their opinions of the parties and their policies. To say that those concerns and opinions are not independent of the parties themselves is not at all to say that they can be easily changed. The electorate is not infinitely malleable, and neither is there an inherent socialist majority hidden somewhere within it. It is simply not the case that Labour can win support for the 'socialist' policies favoured by the left if only it shouts long and hard enough. Many popular concerns will prove extremely resistant to attempts by Labour, or the left within it, to change them – and it would be foolish for a party concerned for its electoral viability to pretend otherwise. I am not concerned here simply to indulge in the ritual left denunciation of the media. Media bias there certainly is and its importance is undeniable, although impact is more complex than left analyses are gener prepared to recognize. There is little prospect of this bias being radically transformed and it will take far more than its denunciation and decisions at Labour Conferences to overcome its effects. In any event, the lack of support for many of Labour's policy positions and the unpopularity of the unions can hardly be ascribed to the media alone. Both Labour and the Conservatives have established for themselves a record in government, the electoral consequences of which will be difficult for them to live down. In the area of economic policy, for example, the chronic failures of both parties in government have undoubtedly contributed to the fall in their joint share of electoral support (Alt, 1979; Butler and Stokes, 1974), and their antics in both government and opposition have done much to undermine popular belief in economic planning, incomes policies, and more generally, in the capacity of British governments to manage the economy (Lereuz, 1976; Stewart, 1978). The credibility of Labour policies in this area may not be helped by the media, but it would be foolish to ascribe Labour's problems to media bias alone.

But the important point to notice with regard to the field of popular concerns and opinions is that it is affected by a variety of interventions, campaigns and ideologies, so that the Labour Party is very far from being the only agency to make significant interventions within it. The outcome of attempts by the Labour Party, or by any other organization, to change popular attitudes cannot be guaranteed, for it will always depend in part on the practices of other political agencies. For example, there has long been evidence of union unpopularity within the electorate, even amongst Labour supporters and union members themselves. But it is clear that the electoral problems arising out of Labour's links with the unions cannot be resolved by the Labour Party alone. They depend not only on the ability of the Conservatives and especially the SDP to exploit those links to Labour's disadvantage, but also on the behaviour and organization of the unions themselves and the TUC, and on their relations with the Labour Party. It is not inevitable that Labour's close ties with the unions should be an electoral obstacle. Labour's ability to claim a special relationship with the unions in 1974 was an electoral advantage, and the weakness of that claim after the debacle of the 1978-9 'winter of discontent' was a factor in Labour's 1979 defeat. Effective union support and cooperation is crucial to the credibility of Labour's policy proposals in the area of economic management.

It is clear, then, that little follows directly from an acknowledgment of the importance of party images and of the concerns and opinions of voters. The field of popular concerns is structured by the influence of numerous agencies and ideologies, many of which will be beyond the capacity of the Labour Party to alter or counteract in the short or medium term. Consideration of how Labour might take account of popular concerns must bring questions of political priorities and objectives together with questions of the organizational capacities of the party, the constraints it operates under and the room for manoeuvre open to it, and of the limits within which electoral concerns might be open to change. These questions will not be easy to answer, they will involve matters of political dispute within the party, a variety of imponderables, and conclusions that are often unpalatable to many on the left.

# Conclusion: Socialism and electoral politics

My aim in this book has been to identify some crucial limitations in the dominant conceptions of socialist politics in Britain today and to indicate some of the ways in which socialist political analysis and strategic thinking needs to be reconstructed. The arguments of the book move from general questions of political analysis under conditions of parliamentary democracy in the first two chapters to questions of socialist strategy in the remaining chapters, concentrating on the principal arguments involved in the non-insurrectionary socialist politics adopted by much of the Labour Party and trades union left.

## Parliamentary democracy

To take the general issues first, Marxism and Parliamentary Democracy (ch.1) considered two major marxist debates on socialist politics under conditions of parliamentary democracy, between Bernstein and Kautsky on the one hand and between Kautsky and Lenin on the other. This chapter aimed to bring out general problems with marxism as a mode of political analysis, especially in connection with the supposed relationships between classes and their interests on the one hand and the institutional conditions of parliamentary democracy on the other, and to establish the weaknesses of both the 'revolutionary' argument that the parliamentary state must be smashed and the 'reformist' arguments for a parliamentary road to socialism. In their different ways the positions of Bernstein, Kautsky and Lenin all suffer from a problem that is endemic to marxist political analysis.

On the one hand marxism regards the organizations, ideologies and institutional forms of political life as different from and irreducible to the economy, classes and their interests, and on the other it insists that the economy plays the ultimately determining rule in society. The problem, often disguised by slogans of 'relative autonomy' or 'determination in the last instance', is that these positions cannot be coherently combined. To the extent that marxist political analysis is predicated on some evasion of that problem it is in constant danger of neglecting the specificity of particular struggles and the forces engaged in them by dissolving them into classes, or class factions, and their supposed interests. I have argued that political analyses conducted in terms of imageries of class struggle and economic determination are highly problematic, whether the imagery in question be that of Kautsky or Lenin or one of the all too many others on offer in contemporary marxism. Support for socialism has to be constructed out of existing popular concerns, movements and organizations. There are no 'natural' constituencies for socialism, as marxist class analysis suggests, and socialists cannot afford to rely for their support on the workings of capitalism or its crises.

Nevertheless, there is more to the arguments of Bernstein, Kautsky and Lenin than their various evasions of the problems of marxist reductionism. They also raise important issues, taken up again in the following chapter, concerning relations between parliament and the state apparatuses on the one hand and between parliament and the electorate on the other. 'Democracy and parliamentary democratic politics' (ch.2) criticized democratic analysis conducted in terms of a notion of sovereignty, proposing instead to analyse democracy in terms of mechanisms of appointment and decision and the conditions in which those mechanisms operate. Reference to the sovereignty of parliament obscures the extent to which governmental appointments and decisions are not made by democratic mechanisms at all, and for that reason it tends to evade the question of the other significant determinants of those decisions. Displacement of the notion of sovereignty therefore opens the way to analysis of supposedly democratic processes in terms of their specific determinations and limitations. I argued that the assessment of supposedly democratic mechanisms is unavoidably controversial. There is no one dimension along which different mechanisms can be unambiguously ranked as being more or less democratic, and any serious evaluation of particular democratic mechanisms will always involve considerations that cannot be derived from the principle of democracy alone. This last point is particularly important in relation to proposals for proportional representation in British parliamentary elections and to Labour left discussions of democratization of the Labour Party and its supposed effects.

As for parliamentary democracy, these arguments imply that the democratic mechanisms of a parliamentary state should be analysed in terms of their scope and organization and their interactions with other determinants of the actions of the state apparatuses, rather than in terms of their supposed articulation of some sovereign will. I have argued that the scope of specifically democratic mechanisms in Britain, as in other parliamentary regimes, is extremely limited. Most decisions and appointments made within the state apparatuses lie outside the scope of democratic mechanisms. This is not at all to say that parliament is an irrelevance, a mere talking shop or an ideological facade for capitalist domination, but it is to say that democratic mechanisms have a definite but limited scope within the state and that it is important to be clear about those limitations and their consequences. Discussion of some of the more striking limitations on the scope of parliamentary democracy in

Britain showed that the limitations are extremely heterogeneous in character both with regard to their mode of operation and the obstacles they present to democratic control. They derive variously from the particular organization of the division of labour between parliament and executive apparatuses, from the specific character of the constitution in which parliamentary mechanisms operate, and from the extent to which significant decisions in areas of social and economic policy are effectively left in private hands. To describe a state as a parliamentary democracy is to say very little about how the state apparatuses work, the political forces that operate on or within them, or the most significant determinants of their actions. These questions require investigations of the workings of specific states and their machinery. They cannot be answered by deduction from the parliamentary character of the state or the capitalist character of its economy.

Now, the heterogeneous character of the limitations on the scope of parliamentary democracy in Britain suggests that there is no reason to confine proposals for democratization to any one type or area of reform. There is certainly room for improvement in parliamentary and electoral mechanisms and for strengthening the role of parliament within the state. But whatever improvements may be introduced at those levels there nevertheless remain important and inescapable limitations on the capacity of parliament to supervise the practices of the state apparatuses. This point follows directly from the division of labour between parliament, which issues decrees, laws and instructions, and the various state apparatuses which are supposed to put them into effect. Parliaments may have at their disposal powerful instruments of control over particular state apparatuses and of investigation into their practices, but it would be foolish to deny their limitations, the opportunities they provide for evasion or misdirection, or to pretend that they can effectively supervise more than a very small part of the activities of the state. It follows that there are important respects in which non-parliamentary mechanisms must play a part in democratic control over the state apparatuses.

I stress this point for it can easily be obscured by the doctrine of the sovereignty of parliament, which regards the problems of democratic control as ultimately a matter for parliament alone. I have shown that this doctrine plays an important part in some of Tony Benn's arguments, but a more disturbing index of its hold over Labour Party thinking appeared as I was preparing this conclusion, in the shape of Michael Foot's condemnation of Peter Tatchell and the refusal of the party's organization committee to endorse him as parliamentary candidate in Bermondsey. Tatchell's crime was to publish an article in *London Labour Briefing* insisting on the limitations of parliamentary and electoral politics and on the need to develop forms of extra-parliamentary politics involving mass popular participation. It is not a well-argued piece, indulging in far too much sloganizing, but it does express a position widely shared by party activists and publicly advocated by other prospective parliamentary candidates and not a few labour MPs. Foot and his supporters on this issue present it as a matter of drawing the line between socialists committed to parliamentary democracy and socialists who are not. It would be foolish to deny that some on the left are hostile to parliamentary democracy, and equally foolish to exaggerate their significance in Labour Party politics. But there will be many others who find themselves placed on the wrong side of the line by Foot's condemnation without in any way rejecting a parliamentary road to socialism in Britain. Why Tatchell should be singled out for such disgraceful treatment is a question that need not concern us here, but it is important to be clear what form of political analysis is at work in the condemnation of his position.

Foot presents a simple choice between commitment to parliamentary democracy and rejection of popular politics on the one hand and commitment to popular politics and hostility to parliamentary democracy on the other (Foot, 1982). There are no good reasons for accepting that crude dichotomy, for what is at stake in Foot's position is the doctrine of the sovereignty of parliament. If that doctrine is accepted then to advocate popular politics is really to challenge the sovereignty of parliament, for it is inevitable that popular politics will sometimes come into conflict with policies of the democratically elected central government. On this view there is nothing wrong with extra-parliamentary politics as a means of displaying the strength (or weakness) of popular feeling on particular issues, but it should go no further than that. I have argued that this view fails to take account of the limitations on effective democratic control within the institutional forms of parliamentary government. To condemn the call for popular politics in the name of the sovereignty of parliament is to say, in effect, that democratic control should be confined within those limitations.

My point here is not at all to suggest that the relationships between parliamentary and extra-parliamentary politics are unproblematic. Quite the contrary. There may well be, for example, conflicts between attempts within the Labour Party to develop its involvement in extra-parliamentary struggles and its electoral strategies. My point rather is to argue that consideration of those relationships cannot be usefully conducted in terms of the notion of sovereignty. Once that notion is discarded as a tool of political analysis then there need be no contradiction in insisting on both the importance of parliamentary and electoral politics as fundamental arenas of social decision making, and on the significance of their limitations for any serious concern with the extension of democratic control over the practices of the state apparatuses. There would certainly be conflicts between any organs of popular democracy that may develop and central government, just as there are from time-to-time between central and local government or, say, between government and trades unions. But that is no reason for opposing extra-parliamentary politics. The possibility of conflict between parliament and other organs of democratic control cannot be avoided without seriously reducing the overall level of democratic control over the apparatuses of government.

## Questions of socialist strategy

The remaining chapters take up some of the implications of the arguments above for the dominant conceptions of socialist politics in Britain today. They are concerned with the non-insurrectionary socialism of the Labour Party and trades union left in which the primary objective of socialist strategy is seen as the achievement of a left-wing Labour government committed to a series of radical policies thought to be capable both of obtaining wide-spread popular support and of providing the preconditions for a longer-term process of socialist reconstruction. These positions usually involve a number of closely related themes, a belief in the unity-in-disunity of the left and the existence of a mass base for socialism that is thought to be inherent in the structure of British society, and a tendentious history of leadership betrayal in the Labour Party, with democratic reform as a means of combating it. The most influential socialist critiques of these positions differ in their assessment of the Labour Party but otherwise share many of their basic presuppositions.

I have argued that these strategies and critiques are seriously misconceived, that they signally fail to come to terms with the conditions of British parliamentary democracy and the constraints which these impose on socialist politics. Chapter three, 'The Labour Party and socialist strategy' considered the principal conceptual foundations of these strategies and their damaging effects on socialist political analysis, concentrating on the notions of accountability in the Labour Party, left unity and the mass base for socialism that is alleged to be inherent in British society. The consequences of rejecting these conceptions were examined in the last chapter, 'Problems of political support'. To say that there is no inherent socialist majority and no general problem of left unity is to say that there is no common project that is shared by all the different groups and organizations on the left. Different groups face different problems, depending on the specific objectives and principles around which they organize. Many of these will differ significantly from one group to another, often giving rise to bitter disputes that cannot be resolved except by transforming the objectives or practices of one or more of the disputing parties. To insist on a *general* problem of left unity is to trivialize such differences. Different groups face specific problems of constructing political support for particular sets of objectives, and this will often involve working with those who may have rather different objectives. But the problems here concern worked out and negotiated alliances rather than the realization of some pre-given unity.

Perhaps the most general problems of political support in British society concern the construction of parliamentary and electoral majorities. It is with these problems that the chapter 'Problems of political support' was largely concerned, criticizing left and right assessments of the relations between Labour and its potential electoral support and the prospects for improving its electoral position. I have argued that anyone concerned with the management of the British economy, with the organization and priorities of central and local government, or with social and economic reform, must also be concerned with the construction of electoral and parliamentary majorities. To the extent that they too are concerned with such issues, socialists of various persuasions have no alternative but to be concerned with the construction of majorities organized around the Labour party. The point here is not that parliamentary and electoral politics are the only worthwhile arenas of political struggle, far from it, but rather that what happens or fails to happen in those arenas can have consequences that are too important to ignore.

## Socialism and electoral politics

Those points are now common currency on the left, though some would bridle at my mention of reform (why stop there?). *The British Road to Socialism* programme of the CPGB, proclaims its intention of working through the Labour Party from without and there are now, as the Labour Party knows to its cost, numerous Trotskyists working through the Labour Party from within. But, if the need to work through the Labour Party is widely recognized, it is a very different matter when we come to the consequences of that recognition. We have seen that the various strategies for a left Labour government do appear to be concerned with constructing parliamentary majorities for Labour. They aim to create a Labour Party working for a programme of socialist transformation, capable of winning majority support because it represents the real interests of the working class and other oppressed and excluded groups in our society. These 'strategies' recognize the need to work for an electorally successful Labour Party, but they refuse to face up to its consequences. I have argued that they are sustained in that refusal by the myth of a mass base for socialism inherent in British society, and, in many cases, by a history of the Labour Party, torn between its essential socialism and persistent leadership betrayal, that is little short of fantastic.

What is at stake in these positions is a faith, which may or may not take a marxist form, in the capacity of capitalist society to grind out a majority with an interest in its overthrow, the only problem then being how to persuade that majority of this interest. In the last resort, history is on our side. Unfortunately, or perhaps fortunately, history is not on anybody's side. In *Marx's Capital and Capitalism Today* my co-authors and I have shown how the view that it is vitiates marxism as a mode of political analysis. Socialists cannot rely on the workings of capitalism or its crises to generate the support they seek. Such support as socialists may obtain for their proposals must be built out of conditions that are not of their choosing and not within their control, many of which cannot be transformed. There are no 'natural' constituencies for socialist ideas, either within the working class or elsewhere. The fact that the Labour Party, and parts of the labour movement, provides arenas where socialist ideas retain a certain credibility is a legacy of the political work of socialists in campaigning, working within and helping to organize the institutions of the labour movement. It is not the result of any essential socialism residing in the Labour Party or the working class.

Where does this leave the prospects for an electorally successful Labour Party? If there is no inherent electoral majority patiently awaiting the socialist call, then it can hardly be relied on to sweep Labour into power. Electoral support must be constructed out of existing popular concerns, movements and organizations. Of course popular concerns are not immutable but all the evidence suggests that few of the socialist policies favoured by the left are capable of obtaining significant popular support under present conditions. The left have campaigned for an extension of public ownership for as long as can be remembered to no great avail, and there have been versions of the left's Alternative Economic Strategy on offer for the best part of a decade, still with little worthwhile popular support. Electoral disenchantment with Labour governments in the post-war period has not favoured either the fringe organizations of the left or the left alternatives on offer inside the Labour Party. These points suggest that the lack of popular support for many of the policy positions associated with the left will not be easy to change and that to campaign on the basis of a more socialist Labour Party of the kind favoured by the left may well be a recipe for electoral disaster. It is important to stress that this is not just a short-term problem. The scenario of a 'socialist' Labour Party possibly losing the next General Election and thereafter rebuilding massive working-class support is the merest fantasy. Without the comforting illusion of an inherent socialist majority the long-term prospects for such a party are

## Socialism and electoral politics

bleak. This fantasy is a dangerous one because of the part it plays in much left campaigning and internal Labour Party battles and because of its damaging consequences, first in helping to drive out of the party, not just a few renegades, but also serious and principled MPs and local councillors, and, second, in strengthening Labour's association with electorally unpopular 'images' (factiousness, public ownership, grandiose economic planning, more central government control, etc.).

The problem for those on the left concerned with working through and for an electorally successful Labour Party is not that of recreating the party in the image of the Labour left: that objective may well be attainable, but it would be a disaster. Rather the problem is that of learning to work within what now remains of the coalition of forces, interests and ideologies that make up the Labour Party. It is to put together programmes and policies that are capable of winning effective support from existing centres of power and bases of political organization, not just from Conference and the CLP's, but also within the PLP and leaderships of the major unions and from sections of the civil service. The construction of a broadly progressive political programme capable of obtaining significant parliamentary and electoral support under present conditions, given the all too evident weakness of British socialism, must involve working with some of those on the right and centre of the Labour movement, and with many who would not regard themselves as socialist. The prospects for Labour campaigning around an agreed set of policies effectively depend on the Left abandoning pursuit of what it regards as a 'socialist' Labour Party. Although I have not been concerned with their politics in this book, it should be noted that in many respects the Labour right faces analogous problems. The left in the party organization and rank and file is a powerful force and Labour's parliamentary representation is electorally dependent on the party organization. If Labour is to have any hope of a respectable electoral showing then the right, too, must learn to work with what remains of the coalition of forces, interests and ideologies that make up the Labour Party.

These last points are reinforced by the formation and apparent strength of the SDP-Liberal alliance. Had the Labour left campaigned differently the SDP may have been prevented or aborted, but there is little point now in lamenting past mistakes. The old two-and-some-bits party system gives every sign of being dead and there is little prospect of reviving it. This fact has two important implications for the electoral prospects of the Labour Party and for what is required if it is to participate in government. First, we must reckon with the strong possibility that no party will emerge from the next election with an overall majority. To rule out participation in government in such circumstances as a matter of principle may prove to be a policy of permanent abstention, especially if the next government were to introduce some kind of proportional representation. If it is not to be ruled out in principle then Labour must be willing to consider negotiating a coalition (or some other agreement) with one or both members of the alliance. Labour should, therefore, consider the terms and conditions in which it might enter such a coalition. But it should also prepare itself for the conduct of negotiations by developing worked out policy positions which can serve as a basis for serious negotiations, especially in policy areas highlighted by the alliance, proportional representation, trades union reforms, reforms of education and the social services, etc. The point here is not that Labour should try to enter government at any cost, for example, by working out in advance policies that the others would accept, but rather that the most effective conduct of negotiation requires a clear position to start from.

Second. at the level of electoral campaigning I have argued that the emergence of the alliance means that Labour can no longer afford to appear defensive and reactive – defence of the health service and education, against cuts, against proportional representation, against reforming the unions, etc. The point here is that where there are only two parties capable of forming a government, then the opposition may be able to win an election with such a posture, but only because the governing party effectively loses. Once the two-and-some-bits game is over, as it now is, then the government losing is not equivalent to Labour winning. This means that it is not sufficient for Labour to present itself as the party of defence against the Tory onslaught. It must develop positive policy positions that can be presented as part of Labour's election platform.

Consider just one example from the policy areas listed above. It now seems likely that the other parties will enter the next election campaign with proposals for trades union reform, and we have seen, in the chapter 'Problems of political support', that there has long been evidence that unions are unpopular with the electorate, even with union members and Labour supporters. Now I have argued that Labour's close ties with the unions do not have to be an electoral obstacle, and that there are no grounds for supporting policies merely because they are popular with the electorate or for rejecting others merely because they are not. But it would clearly do little for Labour's electoral prospects if it were to campaign on the basis of total opposition to trades union reform. Few now in the Labour Party would be so foolish as to advocate the severance of Labour's union connections. Once that option is rejected, as it should be, then it is clear that the electoral problems arising out of those connections cannot be resolved by the Labour Party alone, that they depend on the behaviour and organizations of the unions and on their relations with the Labour Party.

There are severe limits to the reforms that can be imposed on reluctant unions from above. The defeat of the reform proposals outlined in the 1969 White Paper, *In Place of Strife*, brought that lesson home to the Labour leadership (Jenkins, 1970), and it has been reinforced by the fate of subsequent government attempts at the imposition of union reform. This means that the unions could demand a real price as part of an agreed package of reforms, for example, a major extension of workers' role in enterprise management, improvements in the positions of women, part-time workers and the low-paid, changes in social security and pension provision.

It is far from obvious that reform of collective bargaining or union organization need be anti-union or reactionary in character. The right have made much of shortcomings in the democratic character of union decision-making in recent years, but it is now widely recognized on the left that there is much to be desired in this area. It is difficult, for example, to defend a system which ensures that, once elected, the most senior full-time official of a union (e.g. Frank Chapple or Arthur Scargill) has the job for life. There are also cases where reforms are necessary for the effective implementation of policies supported by the unions themselves. The chapter, 'The Labour Party and socialist strategy' referred to the example of planning agreements, supported by the TUC and part of Labour policy since 1973. These were to be tripartite arrangements between government, enterprise management and unions representing the workforce, covering enterprise investment and employment policy, product development, etc. The implementation of planning agreements would clearly affect the character of collective bargaining in the relevant industries. It would also require significant changes in union organization, to cope with problems of inter-union relationships where several are represented in the same enterprise and to develop on the union side an effective capacity to negotiate agreements with management and to monitor their implementation. These points suggest the possibility of turning Labour's special relationship with the major unions into a real electoral asset in the shape of a package agreed between the Labour Party, the TUC and major unions to include trades union reforms, together with serious attempts to develop planning agreements, changes in employment legislation, etc. This would provide the unions with a positive alternative to the reforms that other parties might wish to impose on them and allow Labour to enter the election campaign with a set of positive proposals that stood some chance of being implemented.

To conclude, much of what I have just said will be anathema to many on the left. I have argued that the existing strategies for a left Labour government refuse to face up to what is required for an electorally successful Labour Party under present conditions in Britain. The 'socialist' Labour Party of their dreams would be an electoral disaster, and not only in the short term. Without the comfort of an inbuilt majority, a Sleeping Beauty waiting for her Socialist Prince, the long term prospects for such a party are not appealing. But there is a further important aspect to left discomfort with the direction of these arguments. This is the view, widely voiced on the left of the Labour Party, and underlying the more radical versions of the Alternative Economic Strategy, that Labour's 'task is not to manage capitalism better' (Hain, 1981, p.199), but rather to transform it in a socialist direction. It is impossible to imagine that many Labour voters share that view, and it is just as well for its electoral prospects that they do not. In the eyes of many of its supporters and affiliated unions Labour's task is not to overthrow capitalist society but precisely to manage it better. It will do nothing to advance the cause of socialism in Britain if Labour does not even do that. The successful management of the British economy is an important and worthwhile political objective for the Labour Party, and one that will be difficult enough to satisfy. If Labour could manage that it would be a considerable achievement, one that should not be decried for not yet ushering in socialism. In the end what is most disturbing about the dominant strategies for a left Labour government is that they seem designed to ensure that Labour doesn't get the chance to manage capitalism at all.

# Bibliography

Aaronovitch, S. (1980) *The Road from Thatcherism*, London, Lawrence & Wishhart.

Abrams, M., Rose, R., Hinden, R. (1960) *Must Labour Lose?* Harmondsworth, Penguin.

Addison, P. (1975) *The Road to 1945: British Politics and the Second World War*, London, Cape.

Alt, J. (1979) *The Politics of Economic Decline: economic management and political behaviour in Britain since 1964*, Cambridge University Press.

Baxter, R. (1972) 'The Working Class and Labour Politics', *Political Studies*, Vol. 20.

Benn, A. (1978) *Industry, Technology and Democracy*, IWC Pamphlet, no. 60.

Benn, A. (1979) 'Democracy in the Age of Science', *Political Quarterly*, vol. 50.

Bernstein, E. (1961) *Evolutionary Socialism*, New York, Schocken Books.

Bevan, A. (1978) *In Place of Fear*, London, Quartet.

Butler, D. and Stokes, D. (1974) *Political Change in Britain* (2nd ed.) London, Macmillan.

Coates, D. (1975) *The Labour Party and the Struggle for Socialism*, Cambridge University Press.

Coates, D. (1980) *Labour in Power*, London, Longman.

Communist Party of Great Britain (CPGB) (1980) *The British Road to Socialism*.

Crewe, I., Sarlik, B., Alt, J. (1977) 'Partisan Dealignment in British Politics, 1964–74', *British Journal of Political Science*, Vol. 7.

Cripps, F., Griffith, J., Morrell, F., Reid, J., Townsend, P., Weir, S. (1981) *Manifesto*, London, Pan.

# Bibliography

Crosland, C.A.R. (1956) *The Future of Socialism*, London, Cape.
Crosland, C.A.R. (1960) *Can Labour Win?*, Fabian Tract, 324.
CSE (1980) *The Alternative Economic Strategy*, London, CSE Books.
Cutler, A., Hindess, B., Hirst, P.Q., Hussain, A. (1977, 1978) *Marx's Capital and Capitalism Today*, London, Routledge & Kegan Paul.
Elliot, J. (1978) *Conflict or Cooperation: the growth of industrial democracy*, London, Kogan Page.
Foot, M. 'Statement to Shadow Cabinet', *Guardian*, 4 June 1981.
Foot, M. 'My Kind of Socialism' and 'My Kind of Party', *Observer*, 10 January 1982, 17 January 1982.
Forester, T. (1976) *The Labour Party and the Working Class*, London, Heinemann.
Goldthorpe, J.H. (1980) *Social Mobility and Class Structure in Modern Britain*, Oxford, Clarendon Press.
Goldthorpe, J.H., and Lockwood, D. (1963) 'Affluence and the British Class Structure', *Sociological Review*, vol. 11.
Goldthorpe, J.H., Lockwood, D. Bechofer, F., Platt, J. (1968) *The Affluent Worker*, Cambridge University Press.
Griffith, J. (1981) *The Politics of the Judiciary*, London, Fontana.
Hain, P. (1981) 'A Left Strategy for Labour', *Politics and Power*, Vol. 3.
Haseler, S. (1969) *The Gaitskellites: revisionism in the British Labour Party*, London, Macmillan.
Hatfield, M. (1978) *The House the Left Built*, London, Gollancz.
Hindess, B. (1971) *The Decline of Working Class Politics*, London, MacGibbon & Kee.
Hindess, B. (1981) 'The Politics of Social Mobility', *Economy and Society*, Vol. 10.
Hindess, B. (1982) *'The Decline of Working Class Politics* – a reappraisal' in Chris Cook and Ben Pimlett (eds) *Trades Unions in British Politics*, London, Longman.
Hodgson, G. (1979 a) 'Socialist Economic Strategy', *The Leveller*, April 1979.
Hodgson, G. (1979 b) *Socialist Economic Strategy*, Leeds, ILP, Square One Publications.
Jenkins, P. (1970) *The Battle for Downing Street*, London, Charles Knight.
Jessop, B. (1980) 'Parliamentary Democracy: the limits of Hindess', *Politics and Power*, Vol. 2.
Kautsky, K. (1899) *Bernstein und das sozialdemokratische Programm, Eine Antikritik*, Stuttgart, J. H. Dietz.

Kautsky, K. (1964) *The Dictatorship of the Proletariat*, Ann Arbor, University of Michigan Press.
Kautsky, K. (1971) *The Class Struggle*, New York, W.W. Norton.
Kellner, P. (1979) 'The Voters Who Switch Sides' and 'Not a Defeat: a Disaster', *New Statesman*, 27 April 1979, 18 May 1979.
Labour Coordinating Committee (LCC) (1980) *Towards a Mass Party*.
Labour Party (1945) *Let Us Face the Future*.
Labour Party (1973) *Labour's Programme, 1973*.
Labour Party (1976a) *Labour's Programme, 1976*.
Labour Party (1976b) *Banking and Finance*.
Lenin, V.I. (1964) *The State and Revolution, Collected Works*, Vol. 25, London, Lawrence & Wishart.
Lenin, V.I. *The Proletarian Revolution and the Renegade Kautsky, Collected Works*, Vol. 28, London, Lawrence & Wishart.
Lenin, V.I. 'Theses and Report on Bourgeois Democracy and the Dictatorship of the Proletariat', *Collected Works*, Vol. 28, London, Lawrence & Wishart.
Lenin, V.I. 'The State', *Collected Works*, Vol. 29, London, Lawrence & Wishart.
Leonard, D. (1981) 'Labour and the Voters', in D. Lipsey and D. Leonard (eds) *The Socialist Agenda: Crosland's Legacy*, London, Cape.
Lereuz, J. (1976) *Economic Planning and Politics in Britain*, Oxford, Martin Robertson.
Lipset, S.M. (1960) *Political Man*, London, Heinemann.
Marx, K. and Engels, F. (1970) *Selected Works* (one volume edition) (MESW) London, Lawrence & Wishart.
Meacher, M. (1979) 'The men who block the corridors of power', *Guardian*, 14 June 1979.
Miliband, R. (1973) *Parliamentary Socialism*, London, Merlin.
Miliband, R. (1976) 'Moving On', *Socialist Register*, 1976.
Minkin, L. (1978) *The Labour Party Conference*, London, Allen Lane, The Penguin Press.
Minkin, L. and Seyd, P. (1979a) 'The Labour Party and its Members', *New Society*, 20 September 1979.
Minkin, L. and Seyd, P. (1979b) 'The British Labour Party' in W.E. Paterson and A.H. Thomas (eds) *Social Democratic Parties in Western Europe*, London, Croom Helm.
Mitchell, A. (1979) *Can Labour Win Again?* Fabian Tract, 463.
Panitch, L. (1976) *Social Democracy and Industrial Militancy*, Cambridge University Press.

*Bibliography*

Pimlott, B. (1977) *Labour and the Left in the 1930's*, Cambridge University Press.
Rank and File Mobilising Committee (1981) *Mobilise for Labour Policies*, RFMC Deputy Leadership Campaign.
Stewart, M. (1978) *Politics & Economic Policy in the United Kingdom since 1964*, Oxford, Pergamon Press.
Tatchell, P. (1981) 'What Tatchell wrote about extra-parliamentary protest, *Guardian*', 8 December 1981 (reprinted from London Labour Briefing).
Titmuss, R.M. (1963) *Essays on the Welfare State* (2nd ed.), London, Allen & Unwin.
Williams, S. (1979) 'The Road to Elitism', *Guardian*, 9 July 1979.

# Index

Aaronovitch, S., 97
Abrams, M., 124, 134
Addison, P., 97
affluence, 129, 131–4
Allaun, F., 102, 105
Alt, J., 140
Alternative Economic Strategy, 66, 85–6, 89–90, 97, 151, 156

*Banking and Finance*, 111
Baxter, R., 2
Benn, A., 50–1, 67–70, 74, 80, 88, 146
Bernstein, E., 16–17, 20, 21–4, 28, 31, 34–46, 47, 49, 70–3, 133, 142–3
Bevan, A., 66
*British Road to Socialism*, 94–6, 97–8, 100–1, 116, 150
Butler, D., 123–4, 133–5, 140

Callaghan, J., 110
Campaign for Labour Party Democracy, 104
Campaign for Labour Victory, 103
*Can Labour Win?*, 3, 124, 125, 128–39
*Can Labour Win Again?*, 129–32, 138
*Capital*, 7–9
civil service and ministers, 51–2, 69–70, 110, 112–13
class: and politics, 1–7, 10–11, 17–21, 27–31, 35–6, 70–7, 96, 122–5, 128–37; struggle, 10, 15–42, 143; and state, 15–20, 27–9, 29–38
*Class Struggle, The*, 17–20, 25
*Class Struggles in France, The*, 15–16
coalition government, 153
Coates, D., 98–100
Commune (lessons of), 22–3, 28, 30–1, 62
Communist Party of Great Britain (CPGB), 85, 88–9, 94–5, 114, 116, 150
Crewe, I., *et al*, 123–4, 137
Cripps, F., *et al*, 75, 86, 91, 96, 115, 126–7, 136
Crosland, C. A. R., 3, 9, 124, 125, 128–39
Cutler, A. J. *et al*, 1, 7–12, 40–1, 47

*Decline of Working Class Politics, The*, 1–7
democratic: control, 24–9, 31–2, 34, 35, 42–6; mechanisms, 48–54, 55, 143–5; road to socialism, 17–24, 47, 143, 146; socialism, 10

democratization, 47–8, 52–3, 56, 63, 78–84, 145–6; *see also*, Labour Party
democracy: as a class issue, 23–4, 25–6, 29–37, 38, 42–3, 45, 56–7, 72–3; and civil liberties, 26, 31, 35; consequences of, 48–54, 56, 68, 76–7; industrial, 53, 64–5, 84, 155; popular, 11–12, 20, 29, 32–4, 43–5, 50, 81–3; *see also*, parliamentary democracy
determination in the last instance, 36, 39–42, 47, 143
dictatorship, 28–30, 32; of the proletariat, 23, 25, 28–9, 34
*Dictatorship of the Proletariat, The*, 25–9. 32

electoral struggle, 70–7, 120–5, 128–41
Elliot, J., 84
Engels, F., 15–17, 22, 30, 36
Erfurt programme, 16, 17, 21
Essex studies, 123–4, 137
*Evolutionary Socialism*, 21–4, 38–9
extra-parliamentary politics, 12, 20, 23–4, 80–4, 95, 113, 116–17, 145–8

Foot, M., 53, 146–7
Forester, T., 2, 122, 127
*Future of Socialism, The*, 9

Gaitskell, H., 106
Goldthorpe, J. H., 3–4, 134
Gramsci, A., 36
Griffith, J., 60

Hain, P., 97, 156
Haseler, S., 94
Hatfield, M., 67
Healey, D., 74
Hinden, R., 129
Hodgson, G., 89–90, 108

ILP, 88
*In Place of Strife*, 154
interests, 2–7, 9, 17, 27–8, 36–9, 40–2, 70–6; *see also*, working class

Jenkins, P., 154
Jessop, B., 54

# Index

Kautsky, K., 16–21, 24–46, 47, 49–50, 57, 62, 63, 70–3, 142–3
Kellner, P., 123

*Labour Activist*, 91, 93, 96, 102, 105, 109–10
Labour Coordinating Committee, 88, 93–4, 96, 102–3, 105, 109–10
Labour Party: accountability, 86–7, 93–4, 98, 101–7, 148; as coalition, 13–14, 152–3; Conference, 5–6, 94, 105–7, 108, 109–11, 112, 152; democratization, 52–3, 86, 93–4, 101–17, 109, 115, 127, 144, 148; as essentially socialist, 107, 127–8, 150–1; images, 128–35, 138, 141, 152; leadership betrayal, 86, 91–3, 98, 101–3, 104–6, 114, 118, 126–7, 148, 150; as mass party, 97–8, 146; media bias, 139–40; membership, 1–3, 122; NEC, 111; PLP, 93, 102, 106–7, 152; policy, 5–6, 101–3, 105, 106, 107–13, 120–1; record in government, 65–8, 140, 156; reselection, 103; and socialism, 91–4, 102, 107, 127–8, 150–2; support, 12–14, 96–8, 114, 120–8, 149–56; and trades unions, 3, 6, 13, 73–4, 106–7, 116, 130, 138, 140–1, 152–6; and working class, 1–7, 73–5, 86, 91–100, 122–7, 128–37
*The Labour Party Conference*, 5–6, 94, 110
*Labour's Programme 1973*, 64–5, 66–8, 105, 108, 110, 118
*Labour's Programme 1976*, 105, 110
Labour Solidarity Campaign, 137
left Labour government, 3, 85–99, 100–1, 104, 107–8, 113–17, 118, 120, 125–8, 135, 148, 150, 156
left unity, 94–6, 101, 113–17, 118–20, 148–9
Lenin, V.I., 16–17, 25, 27, 29–46, 47, 49–50, 56–7, 62–3, 70, 72–3, 142–3
Leonard, D., 138
Lereuz, J., 140
*Let Us Face the Future*, 96
Liberal Party, 122, 124, 137–8, 140, 153
Lipset, S. M., 58
Lockwood, D., 134
*London Labour Briefing*, 146

*Manifesto*, 75, 86, 88, 91, 95–6, 115, 126–7, 136
Marx, K., 15, 22, 30, 36, 62
marxism, 7–11, 15–46, 56–7, 70–3, 142–3, 150
*Marx's Capital and Capitalism Today*, 1, 7–12, 40, 47, 150
Meacher, M., 69
Miliband, R., 98–100
*Militant*, 88, 90
Minkin, L., 3, 5, 94, 110, 122, 131, 135
Mitchell, A., 123, 129–32, 138
*Must Labour Lose?*, 124, 129, 134

nationalization, 63–8, 79–80, 109, 111, 126, 138, 152

Panitch, L., 98–100

parliament: and capitalist private property, 63–8; and central bank, 60; and constitution, 58–60; and electorate, 45, 47, 51, 54–6, 70–7, 80, 144; and judiciary, 59–60; and state apparatuses, 19, 26–7, 30–2, 34, 36–7, 45–6, 47,49–54, 56–70, 78, 80–1, 143–6
parliamentary democracy, 11–12, 15–46, 142–8; limitations on, 58–70, 78–9, 144–8; mechanisms of, 54–6; and working class, 4–5, 15–24, 28–32
party and class, 1–7, 17–22, 27–9, 35, 70–7, 122–5, 128–36
Pimlott, B., 97
planning agreements, 66–8, 108, 111, 155
*Political Change in Britain*, 123–4, 133–7, 140
popular concerns, 138–41, 151
public ownership, 64–8, 79, 109, 111, 126, 138, 151

Rank and File Mobilizing Committee, 88, 115
reductionism, 3–6, 11, 39–42, 132–6, 139, 143, 150–1
relative autonomy, 36, 39–42, 47
representation, 27–8, 36, 39–42
revisionism, 17, 21–5, 73, 94, 126–7

SDP (British), 114, 116, 122, 124, 137–8, 140, 153
SDP (German), 16, 17, 20
SDP-Liberal Alliance, 122, 124, 137–8, 153–4
Seyd, P., 3, 122, 131, 135
socialism: democratic, 10; democratic road to, 15–29, 47, 143, 146; ethical, 38–9; and Labour Party, 91–4, 102, 107, 127–8, 150–2; mass base for, 11–12, 18–22, 25, 35, 86, 89–90, 94, 96–101, 113–17, 118–19, 125–7, 131, 135–6, 139, 148–52; scientific and utopian, 10; support for, 10–12, 18–22, 118–19, 125–8, 150–2
*Socialist Commentary*, 134
sovereignty, 45–6, 49–52, 55–8, 62, 65, 78–80, 81–2, 143–4, 146–7
state: as neutral, 30–1, 37; *see also*, parliament
*State and Revolution, The*, 25, 29–32
Stewart, M., 140
Stokes, D., 123–4, 133–5, 140

Tatchell, P., 146
Titmuss, R., 61
trades unions: reform, 154–6; *see also*, Labour Party

voting behaviour, 1–7, 18–22, 70–7, 122–5, 128–41

Williams, S., 53
Wilson, H., 67, 108, 110
working class: affluence, 129, 131–2, 133–4; interests, 2–7, 10, 18, 73–5, 96, 98–100, 113–14, 150; *see also*, Labour Party

162